MOSES RIGHT,

AND

BISHOP COLENSO WRONG;

BEING

Popular Lectures on the Pentateuch.

BY

THE REV. JOHN CUMMING, D.D.,

F. R. S. E.

NEW-YORK:
JOHN BRADBURN, PUBLISHER AND BOOKSELLER,
(SUCCESSOR TO M. DOOLADY,)
No. 49 Walker Street.

1863.

INTRODUCTION.

Numbers who have heard these Lectures have requested the author to print them in a cheap form for extensive circulation. There is a "needs-be." Men of skeptical and irreligious opinions are busy commenting with delight on the untenable criticisms of Bishop Colenso, and young persons especially ignorant of the facts of the subject in discussion are apt to be misled and deceived. These lectures will prove how unreliable the Bishop's statements are, and how strong and impregnable are the truths and facts recorded in Holy Writ; they may, too, by God's blessing, prove of use to such as desire to have their doubts and difficulties, especially on the historical events of the Pentateuch, removed and dissolved. There are various learned and scholarly replies. But these do not meet the cases to which these Lectures are addressed.

MOSES RIGHT,

AND

BISHOP COLENSO WRONG.

CHAPTER I.

WHITHER THE BISHOP'S BARK CARRIES HIM.

I STATED incidentally in some recent remarks that I would endeavor to direct attention to the demerits of a book far more popular than it deserves to be from its intrinsic character, and far more extensively read than a Christian mind could desire, especially by those borderers between truth and error who are incompetent to dispose of its fallacies. I allude to the work upon the "Pentateuch," by Bishop Colenso. Suppose that work had been written by a presbyter of the Scottish Church, I should equally have animadverted on it. It is not because the author is a bishop that I take any pleasure in noticing it; nor is it with words of invective, or in ill-will, or sectarian exclusiveness that I criticise it. It is because the work is doing considerable mischief, as written by a bishop—not, however, among Christians, for this is improbable; but, as I have said, in that class of the community which is still hovering between the truths of the Gospel and the fallacies, plausible fallacies, that profess to disprove or undermine them. On the minds of these, the specious objections, earnestly urged by Bishop Colenso, must have some effect. Now, it is the duty of every faithful minister of Christ not only to feed the flock, which I humbly try to do, but also to beat off the wolf, which I will try to do also. I therefore address myself to the discussion of a theme on which I am persuaded, on the most irrefragable grounds, that the Bishop is wofully deceived; while from all he urges I gather the conviction, that no stone or weapon can be thrown against the foundation of God's inspired Word which can ever injure it.

If the Bishop merely differed from me on some denominational or ecclesiastical questions, I would never think of answering him; or if it were a question that related to the Church of England alone, I would leave it for the good bishops and the faithful ministers that officiate by its altars, to dispose of it. But what he impugns is the heritage and glory of the Church universal. If this Bishop be right, our preaching is vain; our teaching is unnecessary; you have followed cunningly-devised fables, and I have taught—for many years—not the words of soberness and truth, but of error, absurdity, and delusion.

In this lecture I will not enter upon the varied minute and specific arithmetical objections which he adduces; these I will reserve to other chapters. I will show in this, and I think with irresistible logical force, that if the Bishop's objections be true—if they can be sustained by fair and proper evidence, such as a jury of Englishmen could listen to—there is not a book in the Bible that is reliable; there is scarcely a writer in the Bible who is not either a fool or a false witness; and there is barely a fragment left of the inspired records that is worth being treasured up in the hearts, the consciences, and the intellects of Christendom, as a communication from God.

Let me present, first of all, the conclusion at which he has arrived. I will read his own words, from the preface to his book, at page 17. The title of the book —which I do not wish you to read, unless you have the antidote along with the bane—is, "The Pentateuch and Book of Joshua Critically Examined, by the Right Rev. John William Colenso, D.D., Bishop of Natal." He records, in page 17, what his conclusion is:—"I became so convinced of the unhistorical character of very considerable portions of the Mosaic narrative, that I decided not to forward my letter at all;" but, after reconsidering the whole subject, he states the chief result of his examination:—"But the main result of my examination of the Pentateuch," that is, the Book of Genesis, Exodus, Numbers, Leviticus, Deuteronomy —Pentateuch meaning five works, and being the name commonly applied to the Mosaic records—"The main result of my examination of the Pentateuch,—viz., that the narrative, whatever may be its value and meaning, can not be regarded as historically true—is not, unless I greatly deceive myself, a doubtful matter of speculation at all; it is a simple question of facts." And after he has so said, he adds a foot-note, in which he thus explains himself:—"I use the expression 'unhistorical,' or 'not historically true,' throughout, rather than 'fictitious,' since the word 'fiction' is frequently understood to imply *a conscious dishonesty* on the part of the writer, or an intention to deceive." I wish to give him all credit for this. He does not mean that Moses was a dishonest and untruthful man, who wrote a book purposely to deceive and to mislead; Moses was not nearly so bad as that; but he was so ignorant —if it was Moses that wrote the Pentateuch—and so incompetent a witness, and so unreliable an annalist— if, after all, he was a living person and not a myth— that what he has written is of no more historical value, as a record of facts, than one of Walter Scott's novels, or any clever and plausible book of fiction. I have stated, without the least exaggeration, what seems to me substantially the conclusion of Bishop Colenso.

"If we compare," he says, "one passage with another, we shall find them to contain a series of manifest contradictions and inconsistencies, which leave us, it would seem, no alternative but to conclude that main portions of the story of the Exodus, though based probably upon some real historical foundation, yet are certainly not to be regarded as historically true; that, as a whole, it could never in its present form have been written by Moses, or by any one who had actually taken part in the scenes which it professes to describe." He thus concludes that the statements of the Pentateuch are not historically true. But what does this imply? If I were to tell you that "Alison's History of Europe" is not historically true, and if I proved my charge, what would Alison's work be? A myth, a beautiful romance, and nothing more. If I were to prove to you that "Hume's History of England" is not historically true, it would mean that it is a mere creation of the fancy of Hume, and not a literal history of facts. Either the work is historically true, or it is a romance poetically beautiful, but not a record and authentic statement of events. In fact he says, these books which profess to be histories, and to record facts, do not state facts; that the writer, whoever he was, knew nothing about them; that in all probability Moses could not be the writer, for he says he writes a chapter at the end of Deuteronomy giving an account of his own death; and that therefore some bigoted annalist, some romancist among the Jews, some Walter Scott in Israel, must have written these records out of his own heated brain, or from old traditions; and that the history of Creation, the Fall, Redemption, the Flood, Abraham, Noah, all is false, or historically untrue; a splendid romance, but not matter-of-fact.

Now then, having seen these conclusions, I wish to add what the Bishop himself says is the result of all. "What the end may be God only knows; the God of truth only can foresee. Meanwhile, and believing and trusting in his guidance, I have committed my bark to the flood, and am carried along by its waters." Now, I have no doubt the Bishop is perfectly sincere. I think he is indiscreet and rash, but not insincere. He is indeed singularly rash and hasty. Instead of giving conclusions which he says he reached only about eighteen months ago, he ought to have taken the classic advice which he will find in a Latin poet well known to him, no doubt, and have carefully and seriously pondered and weighed them for nine years; and after having done so, as became so grave a subject, he might have published the result of his discovery; but having published it, I give him credit for his statement, that he feels deep pain, because he believes he has thus lifted the anchors of Christendom, and left all afloat upon waters carrying them they not whither, — without a chart, without a compass, and, I fear we must add, without a hope.

All I will attempt in this lecture will be to show you that if Bishop Colenso's position be true, namely, that Moses was not the writer of the Pentateuch, and that what is written in the Pentateuch is not actual, literal, *bonâ fide* historical fact, most of the Old Testament, and nearly all the New Testament, must therefore be equally untrue. I will show that the Bishop, in his own words, having committed his bark to the flood, is carried along upon waters which are wafting him to shores that he never anticipated. He says the Pentateuch is historically false; Moses is probably not the writer. But what logically follows? First of all, that David, the sweet singer of Israel, was totally misinformed, and has stated what is not true; for David says (Psalm ciii. 7), "God made known his ways unto Moses:"—(Psalm cvi. 16), "They envied Moses also in the camp:"—(Psalm cvi. 23), "Moses stood before him in the breach." What would an ordinary reader infer from these words?—that David regarded Moses as a living person, and that he regarded as facts, historic facts, what he quotes and attributes to Moses. But if Bishop Colenso be correct, David—instead of being an inspired penman—was a misinformed rhapsodist; either he was deceived, or he deceives. The Bishop also sweeps away Isaiah; for what does this prophet say?—(Isaiah lxiii. 12), "God led them by the right hand of Moses." He states the fact recorded in Exodus, and repeats it in his own pages, therefore Isaiah was deceived or a deceiver. Jeremiah (xv. 1), who writes, "Though Moses and Samuel stood before me;" regarding these two as great prophets, also was misinformed. Malachi (iv. 4) says, "Remember ye the law of Moses my servant,"—he also was misled. And Peter was totally deceived at Pentecost; for what does he say? (Acts iii. 22) "Moses truly said unto the fathers, A prophet shall the Lord your God raise up unto you of your brethren, like unto me; him shall ye hear in all things whatsoever he shall say unto you." Where did Peter get these words? From the Pentateuch. But evidently Peter was mistaken and deluded, and identified a human fiction with a Divine fact, and probably, therefore, was as much a myth as the writer of the Pentateuch. And not only so, but the proto-martyr Stephen was also utterly deceived on the eve of martyrdom. He said, "Men, brethren, and fathers, hearken, The God of glory appeared unto our father Abraham, when he was in Mesopotamia, before he dwelt in Charran, and said unto him, Get thee out of thy country, and come into the land which I shall show thee." But Abraham is one of the myths of Moses, a fanciful personage, the mere meteor of a troubled fancy. Yet Stephen, the proto-martyr, who spake by the Spirit of God, supposed Abraham to be a living man, and not a mythic person. He proceeds, in this chapter (vii.) of the Acts of the Apostles, "The patriarchs, moved with envy, sold Joseph into Egypt;" that looks like his viewing it as a historic fact. "And when Jacob heard that there was corn in Egypt, he sent out our fathers first;" that also seems historic fact. And then he says again, "So Jacob went down into Egypt, and died, he, and our fathers." And then, in verse 22, "And Moses was learned in all the wisdom of the Egyptians, and was mighty in words and in deeds. And when he was full forty years old, it came into his heart to visit his brethren the children of Israel. And seeing one of them suffer wrong, he defended him, and avenged him that was oppressed, and smote the Egyptian;" that is stated as historic fact. In this chapter, you will find the leading facts of the Pentateuch in brief. Then, what follows? If Moses was not a real person, or if Moses was not the writer of the Pentateuch, or if the Pentateuch be not historically true, Stephen, the great proto-martyr, speaking by the Spirit of God, on the eve of his martyrdom and death, was so deceived and mistaken, that he quoted as facts, airy fables, and alluded to persons who, as Bishop Colenso knows better than Stephen, never had an historic existence at all.

I go farther still; for it will be seen that the Bishop's logic sweeps away every thing that we trust in. I turn to the Apostle Paul. If Moses was not an actual person, if he was not the writer of the Pentateuch, if the Pentateuch be not historically true, what mean the words of Paul in Acts xxvi. 22? "I continue unto this day, witnessing both to small and great, saying none other things than those which the prophets and Moses did say should come." And 1 Cor. x. 2, "They were all baptized unto Moses in the cloud and in the sea." And in 2 Cor. iii. 7, "The children of Israel could not steadfastly behold the face of Moses." And what is still more striking, that roll call, as it has been named, of the illustrious dead — the cloud of witnesses — contained in the eleventh chapter of the epistle to the Hebrews, shows while I read it how thoroughly the Apostle Paul was deceived if Bishop Colenso be specially taught. He says in the fourth verse, "By faith Abel offered unto God a more excellent sacrifice than Cain." What a pity that Paul was not as enlightened as Colenso! He never would then have alluded to two myths as living, historic persons. Again, "By faith Enoch was translated that he should not see death." This looks like the Apostle Paul believing this to be fact. "By faith Noah, being warned of God of things not seen as yet, moved with fear, prepared an ark to the saving of his house; by the which he condemned the world, and became heir of the righteousness which is by faith." "By faith Abraham, when he was called to go out into a place which he should after receive for an inheritance, obeyed." And again, "By faith Abraham, when he was tried, offered up Isaac." And again, "By faith Moses, when he was born, was hid three months of his parents, because they saw he was a proper child; and they were not afraid of the king's commandment. By faith Moses, when he was come to years, refused to be called the son of Pharaoh's daughter, choosing rather to suffer affliction with the people of God, than to enjoy the pleasures of sin for a season; esteeming the reproach of Christ greater riches than the treasures in Egypt; for he had respect unto the recompense of the reward. By faith he forsook Egypt, not fearing the wrath of the king; for he endured as seeing Him who is invisible. Through faith he kept the passover, and the sprinkling of blood, lest He that destroyed the first-born should touch them. By faith they passed through the Red Sea as by dry land; which the Egyptians assaying to do, were drowned. By faith the walls of Jericho fell down after they were compassed about seven days. By faith the harlot Rahab perished not with them that believed not, when she had received the spies with peace. And what shall I say more? for the time would fail me to tell of Gedeon, and of Barak, and of Samson, and of Jephtha, of David also, and Samuel, and of the prophets." Now, what would you infer from this chapter written by the Apostle Paul? That all he records he believed to be actual, that living and historic persons engaged in the very work ascribed to them in the Pentateuch, and that, instead of being myths, and dreams, and romantic representations of things that never were, they were living actors in the world's great drama, and the acts ascribed to them in the Pentateuch the Apostle Paul accepts and reasserts as having actually and historically occurred.

Jude also must have been deceived, for he says that Satan disputed about the body of Moses; and St. John in the Apocalypse plainly must have been misled, for he says the redeemed in heaven sing the song of Moses and the song of the Lamb.

See now what a sweeping issue the Bishop has raised. If Moses was not an actual person, if the Pentateuch be not historically true, then St. Peter was deceived, Stephen was deceived, St. Paul was deceived, Jude and St. John were deceived, then Isaiah and Jeremiah, and the sweet singer of Israel were all deceived; for all these writers distinctly assert the personal existence of Moses, and the great facts of his narrative, as being matters of history; and that he predicted the Messiah, and that the Messiah corresponds to the prediction of

Moses, who had written of Him as inspired by the Holy Spirit of God. Then all these writers either must have been deceived, or they must have written to deceive us. These are the horns of the dilemma; on one or the other the Bishop must rest. If they didn't mean to deceive us (and he gives them credit for honesty), they were utterly deceived themselves; but whether the one or the other, the issue raised by the Bishop is, that his bark, launched upon the floods, lands upon shores dreary and desolate as the Arctic regions around the pole, on which no living thing can grow, and no heart can beat, and no lungs can breathe.

But I go farther than this. I must state also the most awful, but inevitable conclusion to which he impels us. He that spake as never man spake, the Lord of glory, the Prophet and the Teacher of His Church —I speak with the profoundest reverence—if the Bishop be right, was deceived, or has deceived us. If Bishop Colenso's conclusion be correct, I do not see how it is possible to escape this. For what does He say? "As Moses lifted up the serpent in the wilderness, so must the Son of man be lifted up." What does that teach? That the Saviour regarded the lifting up of the serpent by Moses as an actual historical fact. What does He say again in John v. 41? "Had ye believed Moses, ye would have believed me, for he wrote of me." But what does that prove? That the writings of Moses were part of the rule of faith; that the Jews ought to have believed that rule of faith; that Moses was so inspired that he delineated with infallible precision the approaching Deliverer, although an interval of a thousand years and upwards intervened between the time that Moses wrote and the era in which the Saviour came. Then he says again, in Luke xx. 37, "Now that the dead are raised, even Moses showed at the bush." The Saviour also says, Luke xvi. 29, "They have Moses and the prophets, let them hear them. If they hear not Moses and the prophets, neither will they be persuaded, though one rose from the dead." But what does this involve? First, the Saviour teaches that Moses was a person; secondly, that Moses wrote what bore his name amidst the Jewish people; thirdly, that what he wrote was sufficient to show to men the way to heaven so clearly, that they would not see it more clearly if one were to rise from the dead. But Bishop Colenso says that Moses did not write the Pentateuch, that the Pentateuch does not contain literal history; therefore it follows, if Bishop Colenso be right, that the Saviour must have been misinformed, or that the Saviour has misled; and that it was reserved for a Bishop of Natal, in Africa, to illuminate the world in the nineteenth century, and to shed upon all its mysteries, its problems, its fears, and its hopes, a light and truth which He that spake as man never spake did not reach.

But the Bishop himself seems staggered at this conclusion, and therefore in his introduction, page 31, he endeavors to make an apology; but, like most apologies, it leaves the matter not only unmended, but worse than it was before; he says, "It may be said that such words, if understood in this literal sense, can only be supposed to apply to certain parts of the Pentateuch, since most devout Christians will admit that the last chapter of Deuteronomy, which records the death of Moses, could not have been written by his hand." Well, we all admit so much. But then how do we explain it? Why, every body knows that the division of the Bible into chapters is a very recent thing, and that the division of it into texts or verses is a still more recent thing; and every body knows that some of the chapters are so badly divided, that if it would not inflict great inconvenience on the Christian Church, it would be much better to re-divide them. You will find, for instance, in Isaiah, broken and interrupted narratives; an instance is found in the 52d and 53d of Isaiah; we find a chapter sometimes ends with a verse that is incomplete, so that you must look to the next chapter for its conclusion. Now, it is in keeping with this to suppose that the last chapter of Deuteronomy ought to be the first chapter of the book that follows, but has been added to Deuteronomy instead of being prefixed to Joshua; and that it is so is obvious from the mark of dislocation, to which I must ask you to turn, because it will be an answer to the very foolish objection of the Bishop of Natal. Deuteronomy, chapter 33, contains the following paragraph: "And this is the blessing wherewith Moses the man of God blessed the children of Israel before his death." That blessing is beautifully expressed in the 33d of Deuteronomy, closing with the sublime words, "Happy art thou, O Israel; who is like unto thee, O people saved by the Lord, the shield of thy help, and who is the sword of thy excellency? and thine enemies shall be found liars unto thee; and thou shalt tread upon their high places." The 34th chapter unquestionably describes the death of Moses. But if you turn to the book of Joshua, which you find by turning over the leaf, you will see there the very passage that falls in with the 34th chapter of Deuteronomy: "Now after the death of Moses, the servant of the Lord, it came to pass that the Lord spake unto Joshua," implying that the writer of the book of Joshua had previously given an account of the death of his servant Moses. And therefore this 34th chapter of Deuteronomy is really the first chapter of the book of Joshua, and the first must be the second chapter of that book. The misplacement of a chapter should not be made the foundation of so grave a charge.

He says in the next place, "But secondly, and more generally, it may be said that, in making use of such expressions, our Lord did but accommodate His words to the current popular language of the day, as when He speaks, for instance, of God making His sun to rise." He says, "Our Lord did but accommodate His words to the current popular language of the day." Can any one believe that? If He accommodated His words to the popular language of the day, what does our Lord mean by quoting the prophecy, "A prophet shall the Lord your God raise up like unto me from among your brethren; Him shall ye hear in all things?" If that did not refer to our Lord, then it was unjustifiable untruth to say that it did so; if it did refer to our Lord, then it is irresistible proof that Moses, a person, actually so said, and that what he said is so far inspired record. But the popular belief of the day, instead of favoring what the Saviour taught, ran cross to it; and to have accommodated His language to the popular notions of the day would have been to have spoken just the reverse of what He actually spoke; for the whole belief of the day was against what He claimed to be, and hostile to what He taught; and because He so taught they crucified Him; and because He would not accommodate His words, and the words of Moses, to the popular language of the day, but speak forth the words of everlasting truth, they shouted with a national voice, "Not this man, but Barabbas," and they crucified Him between two thieves.

But Bishop Colenso goes farther. He says, "It is not to be supposed that Jesus in His human nature was acquainted, more than any educated Jew of the age, with all the mysteries of all modern science; nor, with St. Luke's expressions before us, can it be seriously maintained that, as an infant, or young child, He possessed a knowledge surpassing that of most of the pious and learned adults of the Hebrew nation upon the subject of the authorship and nature of the different parts of the Pentateuch." Now, let us see what this language implies. He says that Jesus increased in wisdom as He grew in stature; this is unquestionably true. But the question before us is not what Jesus knew as an infant, or whether He was more enlightened as a child than Hebrew adults, but what He was when He stood forth in the midst of the world, the great Teacher, the only Priest, the supreme King of His Church. If He knew no more at thirty years of age, when He assumed the great functions of the infallible and universal Teacher, than the Hebrew adults, His cotemporaries, what have we left us to rely upon? What He taught as the resurrection of the dead, if the Bishop be right, may be a myth; what He taught as pardon of sins through His precious blood, may be a mistake; when He taught the immortality of the soul and the hopes of glory, he may have taught delusions. The Bishop must sink into Socinianism, but he can not stop even there; his bark, that is afloat upon the floods, must carry him to shores more desert, and more distant still. If Jesus was not the perfect Teacher of perfect truth when He taught in the synagogue and on the streets of Jerusalem, He was not the perfect Priest, nor the perfect Sacrifice, nor the perfect Atonement. The anchors of our faith are lifted; Christendom is afloat upon a stormy, dreary, and tempestuous sea; and either the Bishop is ignorant, rash, and reckless, or the Saviour was deceived, or has deceived us. That is the issue he himself has raised, and there is no other conclusion to which it is possible for us to come.

Such, then, is the necessary result of the teaching of Bishop Colenso. He himself seems to have anticipated it, for he admits the possibility of people regarding all in this light. If Bishop Colenso's position be right, that the Pentateuch is not true, that Moses did not write it, or that whoever did write it knew nothing of the facts of the case, and took no part in the incidents recorded in it; then I say Isaiah, Jeremiah, Malachi, David, John, Peter, Stephen, St. Paul, and last and not least, the Lord of glory, were deceived and deluded also.

The Bishop adds, at page 152, when he is looking back at the shores to which his bark has carried him, "The results of scientific criticism"—I call them in this instance the results of episcopal delusion and folly —"the results of scientific criticism applied to the examination of the letter of the Scriptures will also soon be acknowledged as facts"—I believe that every sane man will acknowledge these words to be whims—"which must be laid as the basis of all sound religious teaching." Further he adds, "In view of this change, which I believe is near at hand, and in order to avert the shock which our children's faith must otherwise experience when they find, as they certainly will before long, that the Bible can no longer be regarded as infallibly true in matters of common history." He anticipates the shock that will be felt by our children when they hear a Bishop of the Church of England state that the Scripture can no longer be regarded as infallibly true in matters of common history. Then you ask, does he retain any thing of Christianity at all? He says, "Let us teach the children to look for the sign of God's Spirit speaking to them in the Bible, in that of which their own hearts alone can be the judges, of which the heart of the simple child can judge as well, and often, alas! better than that of the self-willed philosopher, critic, or sage."

He teaches that there are bits of the Bible which are revelations of the Infinite, but that these bits of the Bible each man must discern and select for himself; in other words, that the rule of faith is the intellect and conscience of the individual reader within, not the law and the testimony, the written and inspired record of God without. But if it be true that the heart of man is corrupt; if it be true that conscience itself is debilitated, diseased, and weakened, then it is obvious that man will select as most inspired that portion of the Scriptures which best dovetails with his foregone conclusions. The thief will justify his dishonesty, the licentious man his iniquity, the sinner his guilt; and left to pick and choose the portions that we may think inspired, we shall select the portions (for such is the actual depravity of the human heart) that most completely fall in with our own condition, our conscious condition, in the sight of God, and we shall believe those bits to be inspired which suit our taste, and accommodate our passions, and minister to our lusts, apparently in the greatest fullness and with greatest ease. In other words, if I may judge of Bishop Colenso's conclusion, it is this: that just as nature contains in it traces of a God, though covered by the stain of sin, so the Bible has in it fragments of the truth of God, which every individual must select for himself, and accept or reject according as his own prejudices and passions dictate. In other words, Bishop Colenso plays into the hands of Bishop Wiseman, so that it is not improbable that the two bishops will shake hands, and logically row together in Dr. Colenso's bark. For what is Dr. Wiseman's opinion? That the Bible is a mere heterogeneous and perplexing mass; that no man can understand it, or make any thing of it, or pick his way to heaven out of it, unless he have the illuminating presence of the priest, and the Church, and tradition. Bishop Colenso is clearing the way for the progress of the bark of Bishop Wiseman. He substantially says, "You, Dr. Wiseman, have spoken what is literal truth; the Bible is not infallible; great portions of it were not written by Moses, the rest of it is not very intelligible, it is not historically true; there are bits of it which are true, fragments which are Divine, but poor illiterate man can't be expected to pick them out with any certainty; we must therefore appeal to the Church, to the Pope, to tradition, to the priest, in order to teach us what is and what is not Scripture; and when we have found what is Scripture, to teach us also what it means, and to what it ultimately tends." I have shown in these pages what is the issue that the Bishop has raised, what are the shores to which the waters on which he has set afloat his bark must necessarily carry him.

Meanwhile, let us no less hold fast the teaching of prophets, the lessons of apostles, the beautiful instructions of Him who spake as never man spake; and regard all that has been said by the Bishop of Natal as not weighing one straw against the solemn, the true, the precious conclusion, "All Scripture," from Moses to Revelation, "is given by inspiration of God, and is profitable."

Dr. Adler, the Chief Rabbi of the Jews, thus justly rebukes a chief Minister of the Christian Church:—

"Had the author studied the Bible with a little greater attention, *we* should not have been favored with the outburst of his virtuous indignation, and the Zulu Kaffir would have been taught the true meaning of Ex. xxi. 20—22. Bishop Colenso would have discovered that the commandment does not refer to murder with malice *prepense*, but to accidental manslaughter; and that still, if the slave died under his master's hand, 'it is to be avenged' (for this is the true translation, not 'he shall be punished'). And this expression he would have found explained by the ancient commentators to mean, execution by the sword.

"But, in fact, there is scarcely one difficulty, one imagined contradiction or impossibility, raised and gloated over by him, which has not already been touched upon and satisfactorily explained by one of the Jewish expositors. Thus the prohibition in Deut. xxiii. 12, is explained by them to refer only to the outside of the camp of Levites, and the whole difficulty vanishes. His Lordship may, indeed, claim originality for startling discoveries, such as he makes, *e.g.*, about the Passover. Who but a smatterer in Hebrew would thus pervert the plain language of the text as to make it appear that a Commandment to be observed on the 10th would have been issued on the 14th of that month? But I must not encroach any further upon your valuable space.

"In conclusion, let me ask Bishop Colenso one question. He forbids us from indulging the imagination, that God could only reveal Himself to us by means of an *infallible* book. Will he have us believe that God could reveal Himself through a book which contains such absurdities as he has discovered in it?"

CHAPTER II.

THE FLOOD—THE ARK—GEOLOGICAL EVIDENCE.

I STATED in my last lecture that I would direct attention to a work which has obtained far greater publicity than it deserves. Yet I believe it is one of those strange phenomena in God's providential government of the Church and of the world, which issue in greater glory to God, in good to His Church, vindication of His Word, and eventual benefit to thousands of mankind. Whatever was the design with which it was written, or whatever may be the rashness with which the Bishop, the author of it, writes, I am persuaded, so illogical is his reasoning, so violent are his inductions, that as the result the truth of the Scripture will be vindicated with greater power, and the facts that he denies, disputes, or demurs to, will stand out in clearer, sharper, and more tangible relief.

I showed in my last lecture that Bishop Colenso thinks — first, it is doubtful if ever there was such a person as Moses; and, secondly, it is doubtful if he wrote the Pentateuch, if there was such a person; and, third, if he did write it, its history is of no more actual value than any traditional work subsequently written, or any devout compilation of venerable tales. I may notice — what I mean to follow out afterwards — that the difficulties which beset a narrative are not proofs that the narrative is untrue. You should read Archbishop Whately's acute essay, written to prove that there never was such a person as Napoleon Bonaparte; the meaning of it being, that by conjuring up all the difficulties which beset his history, you may come to the conclusion that such a person as Napoleon Bonaparte never existed, that is, that there was no such person. Now I can prove — with greater force than the Bishop has proved that Moses never existed — that there is no such person in existence, or ever was, as Bishop Colenso — certainly that, if there be, he can not be the author of this book. I say, on precisely the same ground, and with precisely the same weapons, and for much the same reasons, I will engage to show that it is impossible to believe that such a writer as Bishop Colenso exists, or ever was Bishop of Natal, or is author of this book. I stated in last lecture that the Bishop believes his bark to be on the floods, and that the floods must carry it whithersoever they will. I showed where the floods logically and necessarily carry him. He says there was no such person as Moses,— that the Pentateuch, whether written by him or others, is not a true history, — that the alleged facts in it are not true facts. I showed that Isaiah believed they were, Jeremiah believed they were, the Apostle Peter and the Apostle Paul believed they were actual facts. And if you will read the eleventh chapter of the Epistle to the Hebrews, you will see a summary of what the

Apostle Paul believed these facts to be. The proto-martyr Stephen, in his eloquent apology, believed they were facts. But, if they were not facts, and if Moses was not the writer, then Isaiah, Jeremiah, Ezekiel, Paul, Peter, John—all were deceived, or they were deceivers. There is no alternative; either they were deceived, or they were deceivers. But the issue does not stop there; the Saviour expressly appeals to Moses, expressly asserts that his writings were sufficient to lead people to heaven: "If they believe not Moses and the prophets, neither would they repent if one were to rise from the dead." What must be the inference ?—that the Saviour also was deceived. But the Bishop we have seen anticipating such a consequence, endeavors to meet it. What is his defense? That the Saviour was not more enlightened than other adult Jews of His age; that He grew in wisdom, and therefore got better informed as He grew older. That is the monstrous conclusion to which a Bishop, ordained and consecrated to preach the everlasting Gospel, must come. But if that be true, if the Saviour was not the perfect Prophet, He was not the perfect Priest — He was not the perfect Sacrifice. The anchors of Christendom are lifted; as we have seen we are drifting on an unknown and desert ocean, without a compass, without a chart, without a haven, without a pilot, and without a hope.

In this lecture I take up one single point. I will not occupy each lecture in discussing one point; but there is one so important, and which we can meet on his own grounds, that I think it is well that I should keep your attention to it exclusively in this lecture. It is from his account of his interview with a Zulu. He says: "While translating the story of 'The Flood' into the Zulu language, I have had a simple-minded but intelligent native — one with the docility of a child, but the reasoning powers of mature age — look up and ask, 'Is all that true? Do you, Bishop, really believe that all this happened thus; that all the beasts, and birds, and creeping things upon the earth, large and small, from hot countries and cold, came thus by pairs, and entered into the ark with Noah? And did Noah gather food for them *all* — for the beasts and birds of prey, as well as the rest.'" But what did the Bishop say? "My heart answered in the words of the prophet, 'Shall a man speak lies in the name of the Lord?' I dared not do so. My own knowledge of some branches of science — of geology in particular" —It is of geology in particular that the Bishop seems to have been particularly ignorant, for it appears to me that if he had known a little geology, he would not have been thus beaten in argument by an African Zulu. He says, "My own knowledge of some branches of science — of geology in particular — had been much increased since I left England." I fear it must have been a little decreased, or, at all events, the increase must have been of a very infinitesimal description. "And I now knew for certain, on geological grounds, a fact of which I had only had misgivings before — namely, that a *uni-*

versal deluge, such as the Bible manifestly speaks of, could not possibly have taken place in the way described in the Book of Genesis, not to mention other difficulties which the story contains. I refer especially to the circumstance, well known to all geologists (see Lyell's *Elementary Geology*, pp. 197, 198), that volcanic hills exist, of immense extent, in Auvergne and Languedoc, which must have been formed ages before the Noachian Deluge, and which are covered with light and loose substances, pumice-stone, etc., that must have been swept away by a flood, but do not exhibit the slightest sign of having ever been so disturbed. Of course, I am well aware that some have attempted to show that Noah's Deluge was only a *partial* one. But such attempts have ever seemed to me to be made in the very teeth of the Scripture statements, which are as plain and explicit as words can possibly be. Nor is any thing really gained by supposing the Deluge to have been partial. For as waters must find their own level on the earth's surface, without a special miracle, of which the Bible says nothing, a flood which should begin by covering the top of Ararat (if that were conceivable), or a much lower mountain, must necessarily become universal, and in due time sweep over the hills of Auvergne. Knowing this, I felt that I dared not, as a servant of the God of truth, urge my brother man to believe that which I did not myself believe, which I knew to be untrue, as a matter-of-fact historical narrative."

Such is Bishop Colenso's opinion of the Deluge. It

seems, the first discussion he had with a Zulu had a most disastrous effect upon the Bishop. I have read of a zealous Protestant lady, who went all the way to Rome to convert the Pope, and—unhappy woman!—the Pope succeeded in converting her; and she came back a bigoted and thorough Roman Catholic. Bishop Colenso was consecrated, and is now paid, to convert the Zulus; and the real and actual fact, which certainly is not unhistorical, is that the Zulu has converted the Bishop, inducing him to renounce the very truths and doctrines that he went out to establish. The Zulu said, "Is it possible that all these beasts can have been collected from all climates?"—the Zulu forgetting, and the Bishop omitting to tell him, that it is not certain there existed very great difference of climate before the Flood. This is not an ascertained fact—but it is a probable inference. On this, however, I will not lay stress. But the Zulu put the question, "How is it possible that they could have collected them into the ark? How is it possible that Noah could have got food for them?" I think I could have helped the Zulu to a few additional objections and arguments. For instance, might not the Zulu have argued, "How could Noah have built an immense ship, when he was no ship-carpenter, having never served an apprenticeship to the trade, and, as far as the narrative goes, having never been instructed how to lay one plank above another? That must have been a great difficulty. Besides, how could Noah have steered this ship through a stormy and troubled sea, when the mariner's compass was not invented, when there was no chart, and he had not, so far as we know, acquired the art of observing even the lode-stars in the sky to guide him to steer his ship? How could these things be?" The Zulu could have called up a thousand difficulties in the way of the accomplishment of the historical fact recorded in Genesis. But the Bishop, in his answer, seems to have forgotten all the while that God was the Author of the Flood, that God was the personal instructor of Noah; that Omnipotence, and Omnipresence, and Omniscience, were chart, and compass, and steersman to the ark upon that dark and stormy sea. It is easy to put difficulties; it is easy to ask, How could this be—how could that be? We must recollect, the whole of Genesis is the narrative of a special supernatural economy; that it lifts the vail, and shows behind it God in the history and in the acts of that early portion of the human family. If it were a mere human narrative, one could see perplexities; if it were a mere record that man had drawn up without inspiration, one could understand and might naturally ask, how this was possible, and how that was likely, and how improbable something else. But it is expressly stated that God spake to Noah, "I do bring a flood;" it is expressly stated that "God shut him in;" it is expressly stated that Noah walked with God, and God was with Noah. All this is evidence that we are reading a supernatural history, revealing facts that we might easily have inferred, but could not have understood the origin, or the reason, or the bearing of. And therefore the Apostle Paul proved himself the highest philosopher, when he said, "By faith Noah, being warned of God, prepared an ark, and became heir of the righteousness that is by faith."

But let me proceed a little farther, and meet the Bishop on his own ground. He thinks the whole story unlikely and improbable from the difficulties that attend it; that it was impossible the ark could have held all these animals out of warm climates and cold climates; and that therefore the high probability is that it is a piece of beautiful romance, with no foundation in actual history. Let me remind you first what was the size of the ark; it was 300 cubits in length, by 50 cubits in breadth, and 30 cubits in height. Take the cubit on the lowest measurement, though most have taken it at the highest. The word *cubit* is drawn from a Latin word, which means the distance from the elbow of an ordinary sized man to the extremity of his longest finger; and measures, on an average calculation, one foot and a half. Well, the ark was 300 cubits in length—that is, it must have been 450 feet in length: it was 50 cubits in breadth, that is 75 feet broad; it was 30 cubits in height, that is 45 feet high. According to the way of calculating the tonnage of ships, the tonnage of the ark must have been about 40,000 tons. The *Duke of Wellington*, one of our largest war ships —carrying, I believe, 130 guns—is registered under

4,000 tons. I have said the ark, according to this calculation, must have been 40,000 tons; the ark, therefore, must have been in capacity equal to ten large ships of the line the size of the *Duke of Wellington.* What does the *Duke of Wellington* war ship carry? She carries 130 guns. She has a crew, etc., of 1,200 men; she takes ammunition, powder, shot, shell, and all sorts of provision for war, for probably six months or twelve months. She could carry, besides all this, a considerable body of passengers. I may assume, therefore, that if the ark was equal in tonnage to ten ships of the line the size of the *Duke of Wellington*, the ark must have been able to carry at least 12,000 men, and stores equal to the weight of 1,300 guns, and of powder, shot, shell, and provision, or what would be equivalent, for a year. If so, and if it be also true that all the distinct species of four-footed animals can be reduced to a comparatively small number, there was room enough. I need not add that the fish, and a few mammalia, as the whale, etc., which the Bishop, I suspect, has forgotten, did not want a shelter in the ark; the water was their element, and therefore they were not preserved in the ark. I do not think that worms and insects necessarily need have been preserved in the ark. But birds were taken into it, and mammalia, consisting mostly of four-footed animals; and, beside these, we can see, I fancy, abundant space in the ark for two or three thousand families, instead of eight persons—for two or three thousand more tribes, genera, and species of mammalia and birds; and that, in the language of a very able Bishop of the Church of England, Bishop Wilkins—and I wish Bishop Colenso had only read or attended to what he says—"Of the two things, it is much more difficult to assign a number and bulk of creatures necessary to answer the capacity of the ark, than to find sufficient room for the several species of animals necessarily admitted into it." In other words, Bishop Colenso says the ark must have been far too small; Bishop Wilkins says it was far too large. Which Bishop am I to believe? I appeal from both to figures, and infer that there was plenty of room, and room to spare; and that Bishop Colenso, one of the ablest mathematicians and arithmeticians of the day, unquestionably so, has certainly here miscalculated; and that the Zulu has not been answered as he might have been, when he objected to these facts as impossible ever to have occurred in actual history.

Suppose you extinguish the history of Moses, or suppose you regard it as an unreal but beautiful romance, do you extinguish the records of such a fact as a universal deluge? I answer, "No." Suppose the Mosaic narrative were proved unhistorical to-day, the evidence of a universal flood is so great, so wide-spread—in fact, so preserved in varied shapes, that no intelligent man can easily escape the conviction that such a flood some time must have occurred in the history of our world. First, the Phœnician writer Sanchoniathon, praised by Josephus, the historian of the fall of the Jewish capital, the splendid capital of his country, speaks of Noah and the Flood, mentions his grandson Mizraim as twelfth in descent, precisely as we find it in Genesis; and this was written long before the birth of Christ. Berosus the Chaldean says, "The whole human race was once buried, except Noah and his family, saved in a ship." Lucian, a Pagan writer, says, "All flesh was drowned except Deucalion"—the name that the Greeks and Romans gave to Noah—"except Deucalion and his family, on account of its impiety." And Plutarch adds, "Deucalion sent out a bird on his voyage, as it drew near to a close." Here are incidental allusions in history that seem conclusive that it was an extensive traditional belief that such a fact as the Deluge actually occurred. A very admirable writer, Captain Charles Knox, in a work called *The Ark and the Deluge*, says, "Difficult as it may be to fix the exact epoch of this wonderful event, all nations concur that such an event did take place. Traditions of a flood which swept the human race, with very few exceptions, from the face of the earth, have been traced amongst the Chaldeans, the Egyptians, the Phœnicians, the Assyrians, the Persians of times long passed away; and the more recently discovered American Indians of the North, the Mexicans, the Peruvians, the Islanders of the Pacific—Greek, Roman, Goth, Celt, Chinese, Hindoo—all preserve the recollection of a mighty catastrophe;" a universality of belief, I contend, that goes so far to confirm, if confirmation be needed, the literal historic fact recorded in the Book of Genesis. And perhaps if Bishop Colenso had cross-questioned the Zulu with the sagacity with which the Zulu cross-questioned him, he might have discovered that the Zulu had also in his traditions some record of the same great fact of a deluge that overflowed the whole earth.

But the Bishop lays a great stress upon geology. The Flood is not of course to be found in the great pre-Adamite or geological epochs,—there is no trace of it to be discovered there; but I maintain still, and not on my own authority, but on the authority of many competent and able judges, that traces of some such catastrophe are in the drift, and also on the alluvial deposits of the globe on which we now live. Dr. Buckland, in a most able work, called *Reliquiæ Diluvianæ*, —or, as I might translate it, Diluvian Remains, or the Remains of the Flood—refers to what he calls valleys of denudation, being valleys that have been denuded, as evidence of some such diluvial catastrophe; as, for instance, valleys now inclosed between hills, indicating by their structure that they constituted one ridge; and now cloven, or rather the intermediate matter suddenly swept away by water. You could conceive, for instance, a wall of solid brick, extending a quarter of a mile; if you were to see a great fracture in that solid wall, of some hundred yards in width, what would you argue?—that some great force must have pressed against and driven out a portion of the brickwork; and the opposite sides would indicate that they had once been connected. Just as in the great geological epochs —long before the Flood, and long before the history of our race—the sea between Dover and Boulogne, or between Dover and Calais, indicates that the sites of these two towns must have been once united, and that denudation, convulsion, or upheaval must have torn them asunder. Since the introduction of our race into this orb, many hold it irresistibly proved that great ridges of hills have been suddenly struck by some overwhelming rush of water, and rent in twain by the intermediate matter being swept away or denuded. Among the places specially quoted by Dr. Buckland is Devonshire, where he says there are evidences of mountains rent into valleys running to the sea, in which there is no river, containing the remains of animals belonging to our dynasty that must have been destroyed by some sudden irruptive flood. I said Bishop Colenso was playing into the hands of Bishop Wiseman—not intentionally, of course—but that the logic of his reasoning leads to that. Dr. Wiseman, however, wrote a very able book on a subject of which he is a very competent judge, called *Science in Connection with Revealed Religion.* Dr. Wiseman states the following fact — a fact any one can establish: "At Greifenstein, in Saxony, there is a number of granitic prisms, standing upon a plain, and rising to the height of 100 feet and upwards. Each of these is divided by horizontal fissures into so many blocks, and thus they present the idea of a great mass of granite, the connecting parts of which have been violently torn away. In like manner we find the rocks scored with furrows, as if a vast current, bearing heavy masses of rock along, had passed over its surface." Now here is a very striking fact. We find these granite rocks on the surface; and we find them thus severed and scored. We can conceive that an enormous volume of water, rushing from the north to the south, as I will show, with tremendous force and fearful weight—carrying rocks, icebergs, and ruins of all sorts in its waters—had rushed through the intermediate parts of these granite rocks, equal by their position and their strength to resist it—that these rocks would bear the marks of the great rush of waters, and ice, and stones that had swept by them, and scored them with furrows. Such furrows and such scorings are accordingly discovered at this moment. Near Darlington, Dr. Buckland, the great geologist, collected pebbles of more than twenty sorts of greenstone rock and slate, which belong to the lake district of Cumberland; and one block of granite near Darlington, which must have come from the Shap-fells, near Penrith. Mr. Phillips, another eminent geologist, says, "The diluvium of Holderness contains fragments of rocks, not only from Cumberland, but from Norway. In Sweden large rocks occur which have been borne evidently from the north to south." "In America," says Dr. Bigsby, "the shores and lake of Mount Huron appear to have been subjected to the action of a violent rush of water. That such a flood did happen is proved, not only by the abraded state of the surface of the northern main land, but by the immense deposits of sand and rolled masses of rock, which are found in heaps at every level; since these fragments are almost exclusively primitive, and can be in some instances identified with the primitive rocks *in situ* in their position on the northern shore of the lake."—*Geological Transactions*, Vol. I., p. 205. It is only fair to add, whilst quoting these most competent authorities—deriving their weight, not from their assertions, but from their observations of actual phenomena, to the effect that some great flood must have rushed over the surface of our earth—that other geologists, as Sir Charles Lyell, with great ingenuity, try to dispose of these facts upon some such grounds, for instance, as the following: they think that the valleys, such as those in Devonshire, have been excavated, not by the violent rush of some such universal deluge as that which is recorded in the Mosaic history, but by rivers that have gradually subsided and dried up. But we answer—water has no such cutting power as he ascribes to it. Dr. Wiseman will be here my best authority. He says, "The rich vegetation of mosses on the surface of the rocks at and below the water's edge, proves that the rocks on which they grow are not constantly worn away. For instance, in the Nile and the Orinoco: in spite of the vast force of the vast volume of water which rolls down the channels of these rivers, the water, so far from wearing out the rocks, covers these rocks with a rich brown varnish of a peculiar nature." If you look at the sides of a river, you will see that the rush of the waters has not cut nor cloven the rocks, but simply covered them with exquisite tiny forests, beautiful and green—that, looked at with a microscope, have all the beauties of a miniature forest. Sir Roderick Murchison, a living geologist of high attainments, makes the following statement in the *Geological Transactions*, Vol. II., p. 357. Writing of Brora, in Sutherlandshire, a county that I have examined, he says, "These hills in Sutherlandshire probably owe their origin to denudation, which supposition is confirmed by the exposure on the surface of innumerable parallel furrows and irregular scratches, both deep and shallow; such, in short, as can scarcely have been produced by any other operation than the rush of rocky fragments transported by some powerful current. The furrows and scratches," he adds, "appear to have been made by stones of all sizes, which preserve a general parallelism from north-west to south-east." All these traces of a great rushing flood, bearing on its surface rocks and ruins with irresistible force, scratching and scoring the rocks which it swept past by the rocks and ice that it swept before it, and universally from north to south, or from north-west to south—demonstrate, therefore, with a unity and force, in all places, that such must have been the direction of some overwhelming current that may have been earlier than Adam, but may have been the Noachian Deluge. Cuvier, the most celebrated physiological writer, says: "The last revolution that disturbed the globe can not be very ancient. I think, with M. Deluc, that if there be any thing demonstrated in geology, it is this—that the surface of our globe has been the victim of a great and sudden revolution, of which the date can not be much more than 5000 years." Now take all these authorities, the most competent in the world, and refuse the authorities as against Bishop Colenso—take the facts that they state—and the inference may be, that if Moses were to hold his tongue, creation would open its stony lips; and if you disbelieve what is written in the Mosaic page, you may open your eyes, and read what is written upon the stony surface of the globe. The very stones would thus cry out and rebuke the Bishop of Natal.

There is advanced by the Bishop, in the next place, what seems to him a puzzle, that there are "certain volcanic hills in Auvergne and Languedoc which must have been formed ages before the Noachian Deluge, and which are covered with light and loose substances, pumice-stone, etc., that must have been swept away by a flood, but do not exhibit the slightest sign of having ever been so disturbed." My first answer to that is: Suppose you have twenty witnesses that say, "I saw such a thing;" and suppose one witness stands up and says, "I didn't see it;" would you place this one negative testimony against the positive testimony of the others? Now, the Bishop says, "Whatever be these asserted proofs of a universal deluge, whatever be these records upon the stony page, yet there is one fact that is to me conclusive against it all—namely, that there are some loose pumice-stones upon some volcanic hills in Auvergne and Languedoc, which I think the Flood ought to have swept away, but which the Flood did not sweep away; therefore the Flood can not have taken place." But will the Bishop prove—which, mind you, he must prove, in order to give any force to the fact that he quotes—that the last eruption of these volcanic mountains occurred before, not after the Flood? If it occurred before, it would only go to prove what some Christians hold, that the Flood was not universal; but, as he can prove no such thing, the pumice-stone, the tufa, the ashes that remain, may have burst forth from the volcanoes not a hundred, or five hundred, or a thousand years ago. Nay, if the last eruption occurred nearly 4,000 years ago, that would not prove that the Flood had not taken place. What the Bishop is required to demonstrate, and what he can not demonstrate, is, that the eruption of these volcanic hills took place before the Flood. The superstructure raised on the assumed antiquity of layers of lava, etc., is of very questionable value.

It will be argued, perhaps, by some, Why, if such a fact took place, if there was such a vessel constructed as the ark, why have we no trace of it or its contents in the drift or elsewhere? Captain Knox, in the work I have already referred to, makes a very striking statement upon the probability that the ark still actually exists; that in this marvelous age, when the Alps are climbed and the avalanches are embraced, some one may ascend Ararat, and discover in the forsaken bed of an ancient avalanche traces of the ark. This officer writes thus:—

"The whole country about the present Mount Ararat abounds with traditions"—this is another curious and suggestive, if not corroborative fact—"the whole country about the present Mount Ararat abounds with traditions about Noah and the Deluge. The Armenians call the mountain Massissenssar, or the Mountain of the Ark; the Persians call it Koh-i-Nuh, or the Mountain of Noah. It is a common belief in the neighborhood that the ark still exists on the summit of Mount Ararat, the wood being converted into stone; a belief the former part of which has a better foundation than might at first sight appear. The ark, it will be observed, rested on the mountains of Ararat comparatively early in the Deluge, before half the period of submergence was accomplished, and upwards of ten weeks before the mountains made their appearance. It appears from this that the ark must have taken ground upon the upper Ararat, by far the loftiest mountain in the vicinity; and, from the length of time which elapsed before the other mountains began to appear above water, we must infer that its final resting-place was at an altitude great in itself, and considerably above the lower Ararat, which did not become visible for more than two months. Now the summit of the lower Ararat is covered with snow for the greater part of the year, though a partial clearance in summer serves as a guide to the inhabitants of the plain; but the summit of the upper Ararat, soaring to an elevation of more than seventeen thousand feet above the level of the sea, is thousands of feet above the line of perpetual snow. At that low temperature, all decay must have been instantly arrested; wood, frozen as hard and as cold as iron, must have remained unchanged and unchangeable under the dominion of perpetual frost. Even animal matter, as is evidenced by the winter markets in cold countries, will, when once completely frozen, remain an indefinite time without corruption setting in. And we have the most express assurance that the ordinary relationship of seasons, temperature, and cold, were re-established upon the earth: 'While the earth remaineth, seed-time and harvest, cold and heat, summer and winter, day and night, shall not cease.' If, therefore," he continues, "the Ararat of the present day be identical with the Ararat of Moses, which we have no reason to question, Noah must have left the ark—at a period which most commentators agree to have been the beginning of winter—in a position almost if not quite inaccessible to man, thus secure from violent destruction, in a temperature which would render natural decay impossible. So that the simple belief of the Armenian peasants, in the existence of the ark upon these mountains, is founded upon the immutable law of nature;

though the vessel itself is probably still buried under an accumulation of ice and snow that will forever screen it from the sight of man, unless some such convulsion of nature occur as that which in 1840, amid avalanches, and fissures, and landslips, detached huge masses of ice from the summit and sides of Ararat, should rend the icy prison, and reveal,"—what, I add, may in these days of adventure be revealed—"this grand evidence—the ark still existing—of the truth of Scripture."

How startled would Bishop Colenso be, were Ararat to open its snowy lips, as the rocks have opened theirs, and say, "Thy word, O God, is truth!"

The more recent geological solutions of the date of the *drift* I will consider in my next; and there, on the lowest ground, show that the Bishop's geology is no better than his divinity.

I have discussed his objections on the ground that the *drift* relates to and is contemporaneous with the dynasty of man. This ground has recently been given up by many geologists, owing to the remains being chiefly, not wholly, preadamite. Therefore I take up in the next lecture the more recent solutions, and from these I will show that neither a little geology, nor an increased knowledge of it, justifies the Bishop's conclusions.

CHAPTER III.

THE FLOOD—NO DISPROOF FROM GEOLOGY.

I RESUME the remarks which I made upon what Bishop Colenso calls the unhistorical incident recorded in Genesis, that is, the flood, which others, higher than Bishop Colenso, pronounce to be the literal description of an historical fact. I adduced traces of it, not only in the sacred page, but in the traditions of nations; and, as many believe, in the physical history of the globe. I wish now to make some remarks additional to those which I presented in the previous lecture, justifying, on even narrower grounds, the charge we have made, that the Bishop is deluded; that, to use his own language, his bark which he has launched on the floods, is carrying him whither he never dreamed; and showing that the most irresistible logical consistency necessitates this prelate repudiating the whole Scriptures as a myth, and trusting to what he says is the only light that guides him now—the inner light of reason in his own soul. We have already quoted the words which he uses, in referring to the Deluge, in his remarkable volume, which so many have recently referred to. In speaking of the Deluge, he says that his first knowledge of geology led him to believe that it was a strictly historical fact; but that, as he has improved his geology since he left England and went to Natal, he has come to conclude that the Deluge is not an historical fact; that there never was such an event in the history of the human race; that the volcanic traces that remain in Auvergne and Languedoc demonstrate it can not have occurred; and then he concludes by saying: "For, as waters must find their own level on the earth's surface without a special miracle, of which the Bible says nothing." Now, what can the Bishop mean by that? He declares the Flood was not a special miracle, and that the Bible says nothing of its being so. Why, the Bible says expressly that it was so. "I the Lord do bring a flood upon the earth." What means that? He may quibble about the meaning of the word *miracle;* but the Flood was an act of Omnipotence, personal and direct, and it is asserted on the authority of that God that can not lie. He adds, "Knowing this, I felt that I dared not, as a servant of the God of truth, urge my brother man to believe that which I did not myself believe, which I knew to be untrue"—you see he is very positive—"as a matter-of-fact, historical narrative." You recollect the incident; the Bishop was consecrated and paid to convert the Zulu Kaffirs, and most unfortunately the result has been that a Zulu Kaffir has converted him. This at least is plain, that the Bishop not only does not teach what he was sent out to teach, but the very opposite. No wonder that he says, "And now I tremble at the result of my inquiries."

In meeting some of the Bishop's remarks in the last lecture, I assumed that the cubit was 1 foot 6 inches. This is the least favorable assumption. The ark, according to that, was 300 cubits, or 450 feet long, and proportionately broad and high. But, assuming what is probably more correct, that the cubit is really 1 foot 9 inches, then the proportions of the ark would be as follow:—the length of it 525 feet, or about the length of the *Great Eastern* steamship; the breadth of it would be 87 feet 6 inches; and the height of it would be 52 feet 6 inches; and the capacity of the ark, calculated in cubic feet, would be 2,500,000 feet. I proved that it must have had the capacity of nearly ten ships of the size of the *Duke of Wellington* war-ship, one of our largest line-of-battle ships. Professor Hitchcock, the eminent Christian and geologist, says, "Allowing that there are a thousand species of *mammalia*, 600 kinds of birds, 2,000 of reptiles, and 120,000 insects;"—an allowance vastly larger than that which I suggested last lecture, and perhaps more correct—then Professor Hitchcock says, "allow a million cubic feet for *mammalia*," (that is, chiefly the four-footed beasts,) "800,000 cubic feet for birds, 100,000 cubic feet for reptiles, and 100,000 feet for insects, and there would be half a million of cubic feet still left for Noah and his family," forming a very large and respectable suite of cabins. So that when we take the actual facts of the case, the improbability is diminished to the merest trifle; and the certainty of course is that there was a provision, according to the historic record, be it true or be it false, adequate to all the demands and exigencies of the case.

But, in speaking of the traces of the Flood on the earth, I gave, in the first instance, the view that is not the most recent adoption of geologists—that the *drift*, which is next below the *alluvium*, and above which only is the *alluvium*, bears irresistible traces of the Flood. Buckland, and some other geologists, allege that there is reason to believe that the *drift* very extensively bears traces of a series of floods or convulsions, which must have occurred long before the creation of the dynasty of man—that is, in the earlier ages of the earth. But to give you the least favorable view that geology can present, and to show that even on that Bishop Colenso's ground is utterly untenable, I proceed to quote first what Hitchcock observes:— "Not a few geologists," he says, "admit that no such evidence of the occurrence of a general flood at any epoch exists; while those who admit of a general deluge, for the most part regard it as having taken place anterior to man's existence on the globe;" but he candidly adds, that after centuries of discussion, it is likely to be found out that the facts are very imperfectly known in this direction. The first argument he employs against the possibility of the *drift*, as it is called, being the remains and result of the Flood, is the presence of extinct animals and plants, belonging to a creation anterior to man, especially if they exhibit a tropical character, as those do which are usually assigned to the *drift*. That is his first argument against the *drift* being supposed to bear the traces and the marks of the Deluge. But then it assumes, you observe, that the climate of the earth before the Flood was the same as that since the Flood. But, using the word *tropical* in its broad or figurative sense, we may well suppose that the climate of the earth previous to the flood, was far more tropical in every section than it has become since. We have every reason to believe that the temperature of the earth was materially altered; that the very structure of the atmosphere, in its relative proportions of oxygen and nitrogen, underwent a change; and in consequence of this deterioration, no doubt, the life of man since the Flood, as we learn from history in Genesis, was deranged, and became gradually shortened. Another argument he adduces against this *drift* being the remains and wreck of the Noachian Deluge is this, that in the *drift* there are no remains of man found. We should expect, if the *drift* bear the traces of the Deluge, amidst the extinct animals and remains of animal life which it contains, to find those of man. Man's body, chemically considered, is the same as that of the brutes of the earth, only finer, and in better and more beautiful proportion. But they have not yet found a single trace of man in the *drift*, unless it be said that the arrow-heads, so lately talked of, and found in the neighborhood of Amiens, are connected with our dynasty. If found in the *drift*, they would be evidence that it thus bears probable traces of the Noachian Deluge; and if any of the remains of man should be discovered there, so far, and only so far, it would neutralize or dispose of the argument that Professor Hitchcock adduces against the *drift* being considered as related to the Noachian Deluge. But I must ask you to notice that his is at best but a negative argument. No trace of man has yet been found in it. This is true: but the investigation of the geologist has been limited; and to-morrow, in these days of earnest research, traces may be found. It is a negative argument, which subsequent and more successful investigation may absolutely and entirely dispose of. In the next place, the Professor says water appears to have been the principal agent in the Noachian Deluge; but in the product of the *drift*, ice seems also to have been present. My answer is, that the Noachian Deluge is described in the Book of Genesis, not as the gradual rise and gradual gentle decadence of the Flood. It is spoken of in such language as this, "the fountains of the great deep were burst open," "the windows of heaven were broken open"—language surely fitted to imply a great convulsion. And I showed in my last lecture, that there are many traces of some great oceanic movement from the north to the south; the *scoriæ* and furrows upon the stones at Brora, for instance, in Sutherlandshire, and in other parts of the kingdom, proving that they must have been ground against or marked, and impressions left by the rapid and violent passage of hard materials, whether ice or stone. The conclusion, therefore, to which Professor Sedgwick comes, seems to me, taking this last estimate of geologists, the most reasonable. Professor Sedgwick, of Cambridge, one of the most eminent geologists, says: "If we have the clearest proof of great oscillations of the sea level, and have a right to make use of them while we seek to explain the latest phenomena of geology, may we not reasonably suppose that *within the period of the human history* similar oscillations have taken place in those parts of Asia which were the cradle of the human race, and *may have produced that destruction among the early families of men which is described in our sacred history*, and of which so many traditions have been brought down to us through all the streams of ancient and authentic history?" This would lead us to infer that the Deluge is the last of a series of oscillations of the bed of the ocean, not less so because directly from God; and that therefore, so far, taking the view least favorable to Genesis, of geological solutions of the phenomena of the *drift*, there is no evidence whatever against the fact of the Deluge; but, on the contrary, in the language of Professor Sedgwick, very strong reason for admitting that it must have taken place. Hitchcock also concludes, after his elaborate discussion, in the following words: "There are no facts in geology that afford the least presumption against the occurrence of the Noachian Deluge, but rather the contrary."

Now, Bishop Colenso says, that when he knew a little of geology, he believed in the historic character of the Flood; but when he knew more of geology, he discovered it to be an unhistorical and unreliable myth. But, according to Professor Sedgwick, the presumptions of all geology are in favor of it; and, according to Professor Hitchcock, "There are no facts in geology that afford any presumption against the occurrence of the Noachian Deluge, but rather the contrary. The geologist will admit, that in the elevation and subsidence of mountains and continents, and in volcanic agency generally, of which geology contains so many examples, we have an adequate cause for the existence of universal deluges; nor can we say how recently these causes may have operated beneath certain oceans sufficiently to produce the Deluge of Scripture. So that," he continues, "in geology we have a presumption in favor of, rather than an argument against, the existence of the Deluge. And some," he adds, "who have examined, have thought they have discovered in Asia a deposit which can only be referred to the Noachian Deluge."

Now, then, if I take the least favorable evidence furnished by geology, we find that the Bishop has not one inch of solid ground to stand on for his conclusion that geology testifies against the Bible. He tells us, the more he became acquainted with geology, the more he was forced to conclude against Moses. It is evident, that if he will only become a much better geologist since he has returned to England, he will become a more devout believer in the Mosaic record; and that it is not the vast extent of his knowledge of geology, but his utter deficiency and ignorance, that have driven him to conclude that it testifies against the occurrence of that which all antiquity, which Scripture history, and varied and manifold traditions throughout the whole of heathendom, testify and attest to have actually occurred. It is, therefore, the Bishop's geology that is at fault; for if Bishop Colenso had believed Buckland, and Professor Sedgwick, and Professor Hitchcock, he would have believed in Moses; but as he does not believe in their evidence, how can he believe in what Moses records?

The next thing I must notice here, is a third question that remains still to be settled, and which I did not refer to in my last. Is there reason to believe that the Flood was universal? It is but fair and just to admit, that very eminent geologists think that it was not. The late Dr. Pye Smith, the very eminent Independent minister, and a good scholar, concluded that the Flood can not have been universal, that it only covered a little portion of Asia. Professor Hitchcock, from whom I have largely quoted — a thoroughly Christian man—also believes that the Flood was not universal. And the grounds on which he believes it are these: the difficulty of finding food for the animals;

the difficulty of finding water for such a universal Deluge; and third, the distribution of animals and plants throughout the globe, indicates that there must have been several centers of creation, from which animals radiated so far as climate and food required; and on these three grounds he thinks a universal Deluge improbable. But then, he forgets what we never can ignore; that, if there be reliable proof that God has said it was so, that must settle it. Secondly, admit that Omnipotence was in the act, and the chief actor in the drama, as Moses states, and all difficulties are dissolved into air. And, third, accept the Mosaic record—which, of course, the Bishop does not—as inspired; and I think the candid reader of it must infer that the Deluge extended wherever man was. If we turn, first of all, to the seventh chapter of Genesis, where it is recorded, we shall find that the language is scarcely compatible with a limited Deluge: "And the Lord said unto Noah, Come thou and all thy house into the ark, for thee have I seen righteous before me in this generation. Of every clean beast thou shalt take to thee by sevens, the male and his female: and of beasts that are not clean by two, the male and his female. Of fowls also of the air by sevens." And then, the fourth verse,—"For yet seven days, and I will cause it to rain upon the earth forty days and forty nights; and every living substance that I have made will I destroy from off the face of the earth. And Noah did according unto all that the Lord commanded him. And Noah was six hundred years old when the flood of waters was upon the earth. And Noah went in, and his sons, and his wife, and his sons' wives with him, into the ark, because of the waters of the flood." Then it describes the animals that went in: and then, in the tenth verse,—"And it came to pass after seven days, that the waters of the flood were upon the earth. In the six hundredth year of Noah's life, in the second month, the seventeenth day of the month, the same day were all the fountains of the great deep broken up, and the windows of heaven,"—or, as it is in the margin,—"the floodgates of heaven,"—that is, of the atmosphere,—"were opened. And the rain was upon the earth forty days and forty nights. In the selfsame day entered Noah, and Shem, and Ham, and Japheth, the sons of Noah, and Noah's wife, and the three wives of his sons with them, into the ark; they, and every beast after his kind, and all the cattle after their kind, and every creeping thing that creepeth upon the earth after his kind, and every fowl after his kind, every bird of every sort. And they went in unto Noah into the ark, two and two of all flesh, wherein is the breath of life." In verse seventeenth,—"And the flood was forty days upon the earth; and the waters increased, and bare up the ark, and it was lift up above the earth. And the waters prevailed, and were increased greatly upon the earth; and the ark went upon the face of the waters. And the waters prevailed exceedingly upon the earth; and all the high hills, that were under the whole heaven, were covered. Fifteen cubits upward did the waters prevail, and the mountains were covered. And all flesh died that moved upon the earth, both of fowl, and of cattle, and of beast, and of every creeping thing that creepeth upon the earth, and every man; all in whose nostrils was the breath of life, of all that was in the dry land, died. And every living substance was destroyed which was upon the face of the ground, both man, and cattle, and the creeping things, and the fowl of the heaven; and they were destroyed from the earth; and Noah only remained alive, and they that were with him in the ark."

Now, let any plain, unsophisticated man read these words, and his conclusion from the record must at least be that the Flood was universal. First, the fact that the ark settled on Ararat, indicates that the Flood must have risen to the height of 17,000 feet. The mountain of Ararat is 2,000 feet higher than the monarch of the Alps. I know it has been argued by some that the ark may have settled upon the lower point of Ararat; but it even is very many thousand feet high: and when the Word of God says expressly that it settled on the mountain of Ararat, and all tradition indicates—and the inhabitants at the base of the mountain repeat the tradition—that the ark settled there; if this be maintained, I think a flood that rose 17,000 feet above the level of the present sea-mark, or shore-mark, must have been very extensive indeed. At all events, we are certainly within bounds if we infer that the Flood must have been coëxtensive with the crime—for it was a judgment inflicted upon criminals for their wickedness,—and that wherever man had lived, there no living man was left; wherever the dynasty of man was found, there the destroying scourge swept, and there, so far, the Flood must have been universal. But if the discoveries of geology to which I have referred be facts indicating the existence of such a deluge, if the *drift* be regarded as any evidence, its universality must be proof of the universality of the Flood also. But we add, on this subject, geology has nothing to do with the Flood of Moses as a fact. The geologist is simply to read the stony page, to excavate the interior of the globe, to pronounce on facts. And it is important you should distinguish, when you hear men quote geology against the Scriptures, between the facts that geology finds and authenticates, and the fanciful solutions that geologists sometimes give. A phenomenon, or a fact, is what the eye can see and the hand can handle; but the dynamic force that carried the fact there —is a discussion about which men may entirely differ. The first conclusion of geologists was, that the *drift* proved the Flood. If it proved the Flood, it proved its universality. The last conclusion of many of them, founded on negative points—mind you, the absence of man in the *drift*, and the absence of any trace of human civilization also—is that the *drift* relates to pre-Adamite epochs. But the ablest and most accomplished admit, that in it there is nothing presumptive against the occurrence of the Noachian Deluge, but, on the contrary, much in its favor. And therefore, taking this view, and not the other, the Bishop's conclusion, that geology disproves the Flood, is altogether untrue. The following remarks are entitled to great weight.

The writers who advocate the theory of a "partial deluge," not unfrequently urge, as a powerful objection to a "universal deluge," the insufficiency of a natural supply of waters to cover the tops of the highest mountains; and, also somewhat triumphantly, ask what has now become of the surplus waters of the Noachic flood? Notwithstanding, when the speculative geologist desires to account for any observed geological phenomena, he rarely hesitates to evoke some adequate and startling hypothesis—from his Tartarian depths vast mountain-chains arise; or, perchance, Neptunian floods break their "set bounds," and usurp the wide dominion of the hills.

Mr. Hugh Miller, whose late disquisitions in favor of a "partial deluge," are now before the world, tells us in a former publication, and we think very justifiably, that by the power of denudation, a deposition of the old red-sandstone, full 3,000 feet thick, in the western districts of Ross, has been swept away, and gneiss rocks on which it rested laid bare. The same gifted writer also affirms that denudation, to an extent equally great, has taken place in the Scotch coal-field:—"Lunardi," says he, "in his balloon, never reached the point, high over Edinburgh, at which, save for the waste of ocean, the coal-seams would at this moment have lain!" And then he asks:—

"Who was it scooped these stony waves?
Who scalped the brow of Old Cairngorm?
And dug these ever-yawning caves?
'Twas I, the Spirit of the storm."

We doubt it not; nor can we likewise fail to perceive that these tempest-driven surges of ocean, which so rudely scalped the brow of Old Cairngorm, and avowedly rode rampant hundreds of yards above the rocky crests of the highest mountains in Britain, overtopping perhaps the silver cone of Ararat, must assuredly have at least been those of a Deucalion flood, if not, indeed, a veritable Noachian cataclysm! And, therefore, we in turn may well demand, whence came these aërial floods of the geologist, and to whither are they fled?

Especially, we should not be unmindful, that the great Mosaic event was a deviation from, or rather a violation of, the ordinary laws of nature, and not one of a necessary sequence of events; that, in short, it was effected by the extraordinary interposition of Divine power. For the especial accomplishment of His revealed will on this awful occasion, "the windows of heaven were opened, and the fountains of the great deep were broken;" "the waters prevailed exceedingly upon the earth, and all the high hills that were under the whole heaven were covered," the turgid turmoil of waters prevailing, or in other words, collectively continuing their prolonged swell over the face of the globe for a period of upward of 370 days, and then, as continually retiring; or rather hastening before the "wind,"—which the Creator made to pass over the "earth,"—into their "set bounds." And who shall presume to calculate the revolutionizing or transposing effects of this mighty inundating advance, and recession, of the ocean-waters, under circumstances so peculiar, so appalling? Who can confidently affirm that the present wise and beautiful disposition of sea and land was not, in some considerable degree at least, then accomplished through the agency of such tremendous action, and the accompanying signified disruption, depression, and elevation of strata? Inductive science is comparatively silent on this point; it is, in fact, one of nature's hidden mysteries, known only to the omnipotent Architect, who "shut up the seas with doors, when it brake forth as if it had issued out of the womb."—*Holdsworth's Geology and Soils of Ireland*, chapter 8, on "Fossil Remains of the Elk," etc.

Let me show further where the Bishop's bark still carries him. First, it carries him right over Isaiah: the ancient prophet, who sinks before its prow, was so ignorant of the logic of Bishop Colenso, that he says, in his fifty-fourth chapter and ninth verse, "This is as the waters of Noah." His bark must also ride down the prophet Ezekiel, for he says, "Though these three men," these three *men*, not *myths*—if he had said *myths*, I would not have quoted it; but, "Though these three men, Noah, Daniel, and Job." In the third place, St. Paul disappears in this tempestuous ocean, over which this episcopal bark rides so triumphantly; for St. Paul was so ignorant as positively to assert, in Hebrews xi., "Noah, being warned of God of things not yet seen, moved with fear"—you never heard of a myth being moved with fear, or a figure of speech being alarmed—"moved with fear, prepared an ark;" there is an historic statement—"to the saving of his house." And Peter also disappears in the flood on which the Bishop sails with so great confidence, for he was so ignorant and unenlightened as to say, "Which sometime were disobedient, when once the long-suffering of God waited, in the days of Noah, while the ark was a preparing, wherein few, that is, eight souls were saved by water." Now then, if the Deluge be not a fact, how does the Bishop vindicate the veracity, or accept the inspiration, or rely on the writings of Isaiah, of Ezekiel, of St. Paul, and of St. Peter? One or other alternative is certain, and on the one or the other horn of the dilemma I impale Bishop Colenso; either Paul, Peter, Ezekiel, Isaiah, were deceivers, and have deceived us, or they were deceived themselves, and are not inspired; or Bishop Colenso is a rash, unreliable, indiscreet, and misguided Bishop. And if such be the conclusion to which we come, then, I say, instead of being the captain of a large ship, careering on the waters in triumph, and riding down all small crafts that come in its way—whether apostles, prophets, or evangelists—he is not fit to be the skipper of the smallest boat on the smallest millpond in England.

The inference is irresistible, that the Bishop, if right, can not remain where he is. Consistency demands that he should at once disavow Christianity, and say—which will be honest, and upright, and straightforward, "I have been deceived; I have discovered from geology that Moses is neither truthful nor inspired." But, mark you, if Peter and Paul were mistaken about facts, may they not be altogether misled about doctrines? If they believe that the ark of Noah was a fact, but are in error, may they not be mistaken in believing that the cross of Christ was raised on a Judean hill, or that it bore the grand Victim, who has bequeathed to us a glorious sacrifice in which the hearts of millions find anchorage, and ride securely amid the storms and tempests of this present world? But the Bishop goes farther. He who lived as never man lived—He who spake as never man spake, has given a very different judgment from that of His professed teacher, minister, and disciple; for in the 17th chapter of the Gospel according to St. Luke—not Isaiah, not Paul, not Peter, not Ezekiel, but the great Lord and Master of them all says—"And as it was in the days of Noah, so shall it be also in the days of the Son of man. They did eat, they drank, they married wives, they were given in marriage, until the day that Noah entered into the ark, and the flood came, and destroyed them all." Did not the Saviour evidently believe in Noah as a person? Does He not quote the historic incident of the Flood as a fact?—and does He not make that fact the foundation of a prophecy the most magnificent, of issues the most weighty and important? The question is not, does the Bishop believe in Moses?—which he does not; but, does he believe in Christ? I can't see how, if he reject Moses, he can hesitate one single moment in rejecting, not merely the ancient servant, Moses, but the blessed Master, Christ, also. Christianity is the most liberal faith that ever dawned upon the intelligence of man; but Bishop Colenso's is the most latitudinarian. It is one thing to be liberal, it is a totally different thing to be latitudinarian. I am so liberal, that I believe there are Christians in every communion upon earth, and thousands even in the Church of Rome; but I am not so latitudinarian as to believe that Isaiah was mistaken, that Paul was deceived; that Peter was deluded, and that the Prince of peace has quoted as a fact, what was only a fancy embosomed in tradition, and appealed to books, as part of the rule of faith, which have no historical value whatever.

I would, in conclusion, draw two or three useful lessons from the whole. First, where science seems to come into collision with religion—remember the collision is only seeming. Before these lectures are concluded I will bring forward the many instances in Scripture in which the writer does not profess to teach science, but where the reference that he makes covers the most splendid discoveries of science. I will show that whilst Scripture was not written to teach geology, or astronomy, or chemistry, or geography; yet wherever the sacred penman touches on a natural phenomenon, he uses language that covers the most splendid discoveries of modern science. And then, in the second place, remember this, that the Bible rests upon its own evidence; geology rests upon its evidence. When the two, as I have said, seem to come into collision, do not forget that you have already proved the Bible to be God's Word, upon distinct and independent evidence, and you have laid aside that conclusion as a fact in your memory, a conviction in your heart, not to be subverted or swept away by evidence relating to science. Therefore, when you see the two come seemingly into collision, say, "I am satisfied that what is in the Bible is true upon its own distinct and peculiar evidence; and I am convinced that, if there be opposition between the phenomenon you quote, and the text I believe, it is because you do not see the phenomenon clearly, or have not apprehended it correctly; by and by, when you have extended the area of your induction, and are more enlightened through larger experience, we will talk about this collision." The evidence is undeniable that the first impressions of geology were all quoted as being antagonistic to Scripture; and that the ripest conclusions of the ripest scholars are now quoted as proving nothing against Scripture, but very much in harmony with it.

The *Record* quotes these judicious remarks from the "Boyle Lectures" of 1861:

> When objections are urged against any given portion of the evangelical histories, on the ground of discrepancies between them, it must be proved that these discrepancies forbid the possibility of both accounts being equally true. If the objection does not prove this, it proves nothing. . . . Against this "can not" of the infidel stands the "may" of the Christian. We need nothing more than this for the necessities of our position. The assertion of the evidences is that revelation "is" true; the objection of the infidel is that it "can not" be true; the rejoinder of the Christian that it "can" or "may." Thus a hundred different modes may be suggested of reconciling the Mosaic account of the creation with the results of science. It is immaterial to the Christian position to decide which of these is true; it is enough that they are possible.—*The Bible and its Critics*, p. 128.

The Flood illustrates a very important fact.

It is a standing and lasting proof of a moral Governor of the earth. God interposed when the sin of man had become ripe, and showed that the sinner's sin shall find him out. It was a judicial act inflicted by the Judge of all the earth, and at a period when there was no written revelation. Bishop Colenso says he trusts to the inner light of his own mind, though he may have shattered the whole of external revealed religion. But the antediluvians for two thousand years had this inner light; they had no written Scripture; and from Adam to Noah there must have been only three links. Adam in all probability talked with the young boy Methuselah, and the old man Methuselah probably talked with the young man Noah; so that the traditions of the truth taught in Paradise might be transmitted with the least risk of being shipwrecked—yet so little had the inner light saved man from the consequences of his own corruption, that at the time of the Flood all flesh had corrupted its way, and every imagination of the thoughts of the heart of man was only evil continually.

The great lesson that Christendom has learnt from the Flood is, after all, the precious, the personal, the practical; as the largest ships sank like lead in the mighty waters, and the highest hills were overflowed, and the strongest castles were swept away, as straw and straw huts before the Flood, and there was safety for Noah and his only in the ark—so now there is but one name under heaven given among men, whereby ye can be saved; there is but one refuge for the youngest, the oldest, the worst, and the wickedest of mankind. In Christ there is room for all the millions of Christendom; out of Christ there is no present real peace—there is no eternal blessedness for the best that lives. Have you fled to that Refuge? Are you found in Him, not having your own righteousness, but His? If so, just as when the ark careered on the tempestuous billows, when the rain-drops pattered on the roof, and it rocked upon the surging waves, Noah felt secure, not because the ark was strong, but because the promise of his God was sure;—so you, being found in Christ, neither length, nor breadth, nor height, nor depth, nor angels, nor principalities, nor powers, nor any other creature, shall be able to separate from Christ Jesus. And as these floods bore the ark in safety till it rested on the mountains of Ararat, leaving Noah to begin the weary march and the carking work of life again, our Ark, this blessed Ark, built in heaven, will bear you across the floods of time, and in the teeth of the storms of this world, notwithstanding reefs, and shoals, and rocks; and land you, not on the barren mountains of Ararat, to look forth upon a depopulated and dismantled world, but upon the everlasting hills of the heavenly Jerusalem!

CHAPTER IV.

THE BISHOP'S ARITHMETIC AT FAULT.

I PROCEED to investigate the proofs, as they are called, that the Scripture is not inspired, that it is not profitable, and that through it the man of God can not be thoroughly furnished unto every good work. It may certainly be asked, Why should the writing of an individual bishop, however excellent or learned, be made the subject of protracted investigation? The answer is, whatever touches the Bible touches the ark of the Lord. Our hopes for the future are in it; our convictions are drawn from it; it is our guide to duty, and our encouragement to persevere; and all our hopes respecting them that are gone are here also. Take from us the Bible, you shut up the fountain of refreshing waters; you extinguish the light to our feet and the lamp to our path; you take away our chart, our compass, and we are drifting on a stormy sea, without a hope or a haven. It may be suggested, that such a writer will not be noticed by the multitude. His book is being read by thousands of the young; the infidel is glorying in it; those who are not convinced find in it reasons for resigning the little fragment of hope that was in them. Because of this, and not only this, but because the objections he flings against the great historic facts of Genesis give us an opportunity of vindicating their truth, and showing how sound and consistent in all its details the Word of God is, I answer his book.

There are, unquestionably, existing contradictions, if I may call them so, between, for instance, the books of Chronicles and the books of Kings, in a few misprints of numbers. For instance, in 1 Kings iv. 26, Solomon's stalls of horses are spoken of as forty thousand; in 2 Chronicles ix. 25, they are given as four thousand. Seven thousand chariots of the Ammonites were destroyed by David, according to 1 Chronicles xix. 18; only seven hundred were destroyed, according to 2 Samuel x. 18. Again, fifty thousand and seventy of the men of Beth-shemesh were destroyed for looking into the ark, in 1 Samuel vi. 19; in the Syriac version, the number is given as only five thousand and seventy. In these there is transparently an incidental insertion or omission of a point. In every instance the difference is thousands. For instance, in one it is seven thousand; in another it is reduced to seven hundred. In one it is fifty thousand and seventy men; in another it is five thousand and seventy men. In one book it is forty thousand stalls of horses; in another it is four thousand. The similarity of the figures — thousands are put down instead of tens of thousands — indicating that there must have been some omission of a distinctive mark in the one book, or insertion of it in the other; and therefore that one or other must necessarily be what we would call in modern phrase a misprint; namely, it is either four thousand or forty thousand; it is either fifty thousand and seventy or five thousand and seventy; it is either seven thousand or seven hundred; God has not guaranteed that every copyist of a MS. shall be infallible, nor that every printer shall be so. In arithmetical numbers, the omission of a single point, just as in our Arabic numerals the omission of a cipher makes the difference between thousands and hundreds, or between hundreds and tens; so in one book of Scripture there has been omitted a numeral found in another; or in one book has been added what is not found in the other. But should it be asked, How, then, can we get at truth? I answer, the correction is in our hands. Ancient MSS., ancient translations, the earliest and the greatest number, must and do settle what is genuine. Likewise, a searching analysis of the whole story will evolve the number that must be correct. The one book forms the correction of the other. But, suppose the books of the Bible had been written by a person deliberately designing to palm upon the world an imposture, do you think he would have allowed an arithmetical contradiction to occur? If a person is writing a work which he knows to be false, but which he wishes to be believed to be true, he takes care not to say two and two make five in one passage, while two and two make four in the corresponding passage. Such errors never would, in such a case, be allowed. The very fact, that in one or two instances numbers vary, shows that they must have crept in by the incidental carelessness of copyists, and their occurrence is indirect proof that there was no conspiracy to palm a romance, or a tale, or a fable, upon the church, and upon mankind.

In a paper well known — the *Athenæum* — is a letter of immense value from one of the best known and most reliable of travelers in modern times — I mean Mr. J. L. Porter, who has visited and carefully explored the very scenes about which Bishop Colenso speaks. He says :—

"Of late, I have frequently heard the remark made by thoughtful men, that many of the replies to Bishop Colenso on the Pentateuch, are calculated to do more harm than good. It strikes me this is the case with the letter which appears in your last number. Your correspondent affirms that the Bishop 'has demonstrated a consistency in error pervading every part of the Exodus narrative, which absolutely forbids our accepting its arithmetic in the form in which it is now presented to us;' but he avoids the conclusion that 'the narrative is therefore *unhistorical* and *uninspired*,' by a theory which, though certainly ingenious, receives no support from the Bible or from the history of the Hebrew text. It would have been well had both he and Bishop Colenso examined the Scripture passages, and the facts and numbers recorded in them, with a little more attention, ere they charged them with error. I have no hesitation in affirming that a sound and searching criticism will be found triumphantly to establish the authenticity of the whole Pentateuch, in spite of all the arithmetic of Bishop Colenso. Your correspondent instances three points in the sacred narrative which the Bishop has proved to be positively and palpably erroneous. Truth and justice demand that we give them a full and fair examination before we agree with him. The *first point* is, 'the improbability, not to say *impossibility*, of *seventy* souls multiplying in the course of 215 years into a population of about or over two millions.' I maintain that there is no *impossibility* here; and I also maintain that there can be no error in the numbers, because the whole tenor of the narrative leads us to expect an enormous increase. Let us look at a few facts. We are told that a special blessing of vast increase of his seed was repeatedly promised to Abraham (Gen. xii. 2; xv. 5; xvii. 6; xxii. 17), and renewed to Isaac (xxv. 23), and Jacob (xxviii. 14; xxxii. 12; xlvi. 3). We are told that this blessing rested specially on the Israelites in Egypt (Exodus i. 7). We are told that 'Joseph saw Ephraim's children of the *third* generation; the children also of Machir, the son of Manasseh, were brought up upon Joseph's knees' (Gen. l. 23). Joseph was about 34 years old when his sons were born (Gen. xli. 46–50), and he died aged 110 (l. 26). Hence it follows that in this instance the *fourth* generation was born, and *four generations were alive together*, only seventy-five years after the descent into Egypt. We are told (1 Chron. vii. 22–27) that Joshua was the *tenth* in descent from Joseph; that is, there were *ten* generations within the 215 years' residence in Egypt. Again, Nahshon, who was prince of the tribe of Judah at the exodus, was of the *sixth* generation, and *not* through the line of eldest sons (1 Chron. ii. 3–10). We have many incidental proofs that the Israelites married very young, and that three and four generations were often alive together (Num. ii. 18; Exod. xvii. 8–16). These facts prepare the way for a true estimate of the Israelites at the exodus. We are not to form our estimate according to what is probable or usual under ordinary circumstances, but according to what is *possible* under such extraordinary circumstances. Now, suppose that the Israelites remained in Egypt only 215 years: this will give seven generations of nearly thirty-one years each. Suppose that each man had, on an average, *four sons* at the age of thirty; Benjamin had *ten* before that age. Suppose, further, the number of the males who went down, and afterward became fathers, to be sixty-seven. Calculating upon these data, the number of souls at the exodus would amount to 2,195,456. And this does not include the descendants of Jacob's servants, who were doubtless numerous; nor does it take into account additional children born after the father attained the age of thirty, nor the more rapid increase of those born before that age. In many cases besides that of Joshua there may have been *ten* generations instead of *seven*. Bishop Colenso can not deny that this is *possible*, nor can he deny that the whole tenor of the narrative warrants us in supposing an enormous and even unparalleled increase." So that the Bishop's arithmetic is totally at fault in his calculation.

"The *second point*," says Mr. Porter, "supposed to 'demonstrate' an error in the sacred narrative, is the estimated size of the camp in the wilderness,—'not much inferior, in compass, we must suppose, to London.' It is assumed that the whole two millions of people were grouped close together in a camp. This is opposed alike to the whole tenor of the narrative and to common sense. Any one who has had an opportunity of visiting the great Arab tribes of the Syrian desert can see that the Bishop's difficulties are here purely imaginary. The Israelites had immense flocks and herds (Exod. xii. 38); these, from the necessity of the case, and like the flocks of the modern Bedouin, were scattered far and wide over the peninsula, and probably over the plain northwards. On one occasion I rode for two successive days in a straight line through the flocks of a section of the Anazeh tribe, and the encampment of the chief was then at a noted fountain, thirty miles distant, at right angles to my course; yet the country was swarming with men and women, boys and girls, looking after the cattle. In like manner the great bulk of the Israelites would be scattered over the desert. The camp would thus be a mere nucleus; large, no doubt, but not approaching the exaggerated estimate of

Bishop Colenso. Yet, being the head-quarters of the nation, containing the tabernacle, the priests, and the chiefs, and forming the rallying point for the warriors, it was the only place with which the sacred historian was concerned. This view, which is natural, scriptural, and in accordance with the universal practice of Oriental nomads, sweeps away a host of difficulties conjured up by the imagination, and then supported by the arithmetic of Bishop Colenso."

The Bishop, you observe, has assumed that the camp, instead of being the palatial and sacred residence of the chiefs, was the great encampment of the whole two millions and upwards in the desert. He has, therefore, been wholly misled in his arithmetic. Had he studied arithmetic much more he would have blundered in theology much less. The third point noticed by this writer is more important still; and I read it because it is the testimony of one who has been upon the very spots that are in discussion, and who is competent to give an opinion. "'The climax of inconsistency between facts and figures is reached, when we come to the notice by the Lord to Israel, contained in Exod. xxiii. 29, "I will not drive them (the nations of Canaan) out from before thee in one year, lest *the land become desolate, and the beast of the field multiply against thee*," and are reminded that by the present numbers (without reckoning the aboriginal Canaanites, "seven nations greater and mightier" than Israel itself), Canaan would be as thickly peopled as the counties of Norfolk, Suffolk, and Essex, at the present day. It is impossible not to see that on the very face of the narrative a population is pre-supposed widely at variance with the numbers at present existing in the text.' It was with no little astonishment I found such an acute writer indorsing this argument of Bishop Colenso. The argument is, the Israelites numbered *two millions*, Canaan contained only 11,000 square miles. To suppose that with such a population the land could become desolate, or the beast of the field multiply, is absurd. It is further stated, by way of illustration and proof, that Natal contains 18,000 square miles, and only 150,000 souls, yet most of the wild beasts have been exterminated. Here is at once the greatest and most inexcusable blunder in the Bishop's whole book. He takes his estimate of the size of the land from Dr. Kitto, and it is accurate, *so far as concerns the portion divided among the tribes by Joshua*, but that is not the land referred to in Exod. xxiii. 29. Had he looked at verse 31 of that chapter he might have been saved from a blunder, of which he may well feel ashamed. The boundaries of the land alluded to are there given: '*From the Red Sea unto the sea of the Philistines, and from the desert unto the river.*' They were defined before, in the promise to Abraham (Gen. xv. 18)—'*From the river of Egypt unto the great river, the river Euphrates.*' That land is 500 miles long, by 100 broad, and contains about 50,000 square miles: or nearly *five times* Bishop Colenso's estimate! Further, the population of that country, at the present moment, is about two millions, or about equal to the number of the Israelites at the exodus; and I can testify that *more than three-fourths* of the richest and the best of the country lies *completely desolate.* The vast plains of Moab and Esdraelon, and the whole valley of the Jordan, are without an inhabitant. In the plains of Philistia, Sharon, Bashan, Cœlosyria, and Hamath not *one-tenth* of the soil is under cultivation. In one section of Bashan I saw upwards of seventy *deserted* towns and villages. Bishop Colenso says that though the population of Natal is so small, most of the wild beasts have long ago disappeared, and the inhabitants are perfectly well able to maintain their ground against the rest. He forgets, however, to thank gunpowder and the rifle for this. Had the people of Natal contended against the wild beasts as the ancient Jews did, with spears, and arrows, and slings; had the chiefs of the colony been forced to fight African lions as David fought the lion that attacked his sheep, when he caught him by the beard, and smote him and slew him (1 Sam. xvii. 34), the Bishop would have had a different tale to tell this day. Many of the wild beasts have disappeared from Syria, but many still infest the country. In the plain of Damascus wild swine commit great ravages on the grain. This is the case along the banks of the Jordan and in other places. On the sides of Anti-Lebanon I have known the bears to destroy whole vineyards in a single night. When traveling through some districts of the country my tent was surrounded every night by troops of jackals and hyenas, and more than once they have left me without a breakfast. With my own eyes I have seen jackals dragging corpses from the graves beneath the very walls of Jerusalem. Were it not that the peasants are pretty generally armed with rifles, the grain crops and vineyards in many parts of Syria would be completely destroyed by wild beasts.

"The public will now see how very little Bishop Colenso knows of Bible lands, and how wise and good was the Divine promise, 'I will not drive them out from before thee in one year, lest the land become desolate, and the beast of the field multiply against thee.'"

Nothing can be more crushing than the personal testimony of so competent an historian, who speaks, not from argument, but from personal visits to the spots that the Bishop refers to; and nothing can be more complete than the exposure of the gross blunder which the Bishop has perpetrated in supposing that a land of 11,000 square miles was referred to, when, if he had opened his Bible, and read on in the very passage on which he was making such hostile criticisms, he would have discovered that instead of being 11,000, it was 50,000, or nearly five times the amount in area.

I proceed to notice another point where the Bishop really is guilty of a grievous misquotation of the very words of Scripture. At page 17 of his book, he complains of a passage, Genesis xlvi. 12, which he thus quotes, "And the sons of Judah, Er, and Onan, and Shelah, and Pharez, and Zarah; but Er and Onan died in the land of Canaan; and the sons of Pharez, Hezron, and Hamul." What he says here is, "It appears to me to be certain, that the writer here means to say that Hezron and Hamul were *born in the land of Canaan*, and were among the seventy persons (including Jacob himself, and Joseph, and his two sons) who *came into Egypt with Jacob*." But, he argues, this can not be. "Judah was *forty-two* years old, according to the story, when he went down with Jacob into Egypt;" and during these forty-two years, according to this statement, he must have grown up, he must have married, his eldest son must have married, and had children; he must have, therefore, had children, and probably grandchildren: and that Hezron and Hamul were of these. The Bishop reads the passage, "And the sons of Pharez, Hezron, and Hamul," as if these were sons that were born in the land of Canaan. But if you turn to the passage, the reading is not what he alleges. It occurs in the forty-sixth chapter of Genesis, at the twelfth verse, where you will find these words: "And the sons of Judah; Er, and Onan, and Shelah, and Pharez, and Zarah; but Er and Onan died in the land of Canaan." Now, there is a full stop in my Bible at "the land of Canaan." In the Bishop's quotation there is only a semi-colon. What business had he to alter punctuation without a reason of any sort assigned for it? Then he says, "and the sons of Pharez, Hezron, and Hamul." He links them with the rest that were born to Judah and his sons. But in the Bible it begins a new sentence, "And the sons of Pharez *were* Hezron and Hamul." It does not describe them as sons there born, it is simply a new sentence, which the Bishop, almost with Popish ingenuity, alters and mutilates, because it seems to serve a point in his argument. Now, assuming that marriages took place, as we know they did, in eastern climes, at a very early date, the whole account, read as the Bible gives it, not as the Bishop mutilates it, is not only just and true, but perfectly probable and credible.

The next thing the Bishop discusses is the size of the tabernacle, and its unhistorical associations. His argument is at page 31 of his book. He quotes the words, "And Jehovah spake unto Moses, saying, Gather thou all the congregation together unto the door of the tabernacle of the congregation. And Moses did as Jehovah commanded him. And the assembly was gathered together unto the door of the tabernacle of the congregation." The Bishop argues, it is impossible that the whole body of the people could have been thus gathered. He says, "First, it appears to be certain that, by the expressions used so often, here and elsewhere, 'the assembly,' 'the whole assembly,' 'all the congregation,' is meant the whole body of the people—at all events, the *adult males in the prime of life* among them—and not merely the *elders or heads of the people*, as some have supposed, in order to escape from such difficulties as that which we are now about to consider. At any rate, I can not, with due regard to the truth, allow myself to believe, or attempt to persuade others to believe, that such expressions as the above can possibly be meant to be understood of the elders only." Then he says, "Now the whole width of the tabernacle was 10 cubits or 18 feet, reckoning the cubit at 1.824 feet (see *Bagster's Bible*), and its length was 30 cubits, or 54 feet, as may be gathered from Ex. xxvi. Allowing two feet in width for each full-grown man, nine men could just have stood in front of it. Supposing, then, that all the congregation of adult males in the prime of life had given due heed to the divine summons, and had hastened to take their stand, side by side, as closely as possible, in front, not merely of the *door*, but of the whole *end* of the tabernacle, in which the door was, they would have reached, allowing 18 inches between each rank of nine men, for a distance of more than 100,000 feet—in fact, nearly *twenty miles.* It is inconceivable how, under such circumstances, 'all the assembly,' the 'whole congregation,' could have been summoned to attend 'at the door of the tabernacle,' by the express command of Almighty God." Such is the Bishop's arithmetic. He calculates the size of the door of the tabernacle, he counts the number summoned to assemble at it; he then asks, "How could such a vast mass of men have stood within a very small space indeed?" They must have occupied twenty miles; how could they be compressed into an area a few yards square? The answer we give is, that if the writer of the book had meant to deceive, he never would have committed the palpable blunder of asserting that hundreds of thousands of men were compressed into an area 82 feet by 42. But the Bishop, long resident among African Zulus, has forgotten what is called the *usus loquendi*, or the custom of speech in modern times. We read, not many years ago, that the Russians had invaded Turkey;—What! the Bishop would exclaim, do you mean to say that the sixty millions of people that belong to Russia can all be contained within the small space of Turkey in Europe? The thing is impossible, incredible, and therefore, unhistorical. But every sane Englishman understands the phrase, and has not a single doubt about its truth. I read in the newspaper that the House of Commons, last year, was summoned to the bar of the House of Lords, and they duly attended. Suppose Bishop Colenso were to hear of it, he would exclaim, What an outrage upon common sense! How could 600 men, constituting the House of Commons, find room to stand at the bar of the House of Lords, where there is positively room for some fifty or sixty men only? The *Times* newspaper, therefore, must have stated a falsehood; the House of Commons never could have met at the bar of the House of Lords; the thing is incredible and impossible. And yet every sane reader knows it is credible, and strictly true. Alison, the eminent historian, says, that when the great captain of a former century, Napoleon, had assembled his brilliant troops around the pyramids of Egypt, amounting to some 30,000 men, in one of those lightning addresses that he made, he said, "Forty centuries, my soldiers, are looking down upon you from these pyramids." He so addressed his army, consisting, as we have said, of 30,000 men. But the Bishop would argue, How could 30,000 men have heard Napoleon's voice, which was not very strong? we know, as matter of statistics, that the human voice, in the open air, won't reach over 4000 men. But we believe that Alison was right, and that the Bishop is quibbling. The language that applies to the House of Lords, to the invasion of a nation, to the address of a commander to his army, is similarly applied in Scripture, for Scripture speaks according to the usages and customs of mankind, and not according to the hard arithmetical calculations of this most crotchety Bishop.

I proceed to another statement of the Bishop. He quotes Leviticus iv. 11; "And the skin of the bullock, and all his flesh, with his head, and with his legs, and his inwards, and his dung, even the whole bullock, shall he (the priest) carry forth without the camp, unto a clean place." I must remind you, that Mr. Porter says, the camp, instead of being twelve miles square, as the Bishop contends, was a mere central spot, like a palace in the midst of a capital. But the Bishop says, "The offal of these sacrifices would have had to be carried by Aaron himself, or one of his sons, a distance of six miles. In fact, we have to imagine the priest having himself to carry, on his back on foot, from St. Paul's to the outskirts of the metropolis, the skin, and flesh, and head, and legs, and inwards, and dung, even the whole bullock, and the people having to carry out their rubbish in like manner, and bring in their daily supplies of water and fuel, after first cutting down the latter where they could find it! Further, we have to imagine half a million of men going out daily — the 22,000 Levites for a distance of *six miles* — to the suburbs for the common necessities of nature! The supposition involves of course an absurdity." My first reply is, that the camp, instead of being twelve miles square, or six miles from the center on each side, was probably not a single mile. That alone would be an extinguishing answer. But still it would be said, How could the priest, a man, carry a bullock on his back, outside the camp, to a clean place, any distance? The answer is given by the Rev. Mr. M'Caul, a clergyman of the Church of England, in London, who shows that the Hebrew verb, "shall carry out," is *vehotzi.* In the Hebrew, there is a conjugation called the Hiphil, or causative conjugation; and this word *vehotzi* is in the causative, or the Hiphil conjugation; and the meaning of it therefore is, "he shall cause to be carried out." Surely, the Bishop did not study his Hebrew grammar, or open a Hebrew lexicon; if he had, he would have been saved perpetrating so gross a blunder. But suppose the Bishop had not looked into a Hebrew lexicon, or a Hebrew grammar, but had examined parallel passages in our version, he would have found how absurd is the interpretation he puts upon it. I take, for instance, Leviticus xxiv. 13; "And the Lord spake unto Moses, saying, Bring forth him that hath cursed." Here is an order to Moses to bring forth him that cursed. Now read verse 23, that follows; "And Moses spake to the children of Israel, that they should bring forth him that had cursed out of the camp, and stone him with stones. And the children of Israel did as the Lord commanded Moses." The command was given to the high priest not personally to carry forth the bullock, but that he should cause to be done what God commanded him. We say of the Duke of Wellington, he beat the French at Waterloo. Bishop Colenso would say, How was it possible this single individual, the Duke of Wellington, could have beaten the whole French army at Waterloo? The answer is, he did it through the instrumentality of his troops. In the same manner the high priest was commanded to carry out the bullock. How could a single man bear such an enormous weight upon his shoulders, unless he were an Atlas? The answer is, that the Hebrew verb is in the Hiphil, or causative conjugation, and that he was to cause to be done what he was commanded to do; just as when the Lord commanded Moses to take forth him that cursed, and kill him, the Israelites did it;

and *qui facit per alium facit per se*, "he that does a thing by another does it himself."

The next passage that the Bishop quarrels with, is in Deuteronomy viii. 15; which he quotes to prove that there was no water in the wilderness. Now, this is one of the most inexcusable blunders, I think, in the whole of the Bishop's book; and I quote this, to show you how utterly baseless are his assaults, and how completely recoil all the weapons that he levels against the fortress of Divine truth. I turn to Deuteronomy viii. 15, and I find it as follows; "Who led thee through that great and terrible wilderness, wherein were fiery serpents, and scorpions, and drought, where there was no water;" the Bishop stops here. I have noticed that a Roman Catholic priest in discussion, when he quotes a text for one thing, always leaves out what proves that it means the opposite. It is invariably so. Now the Bishop quotes this text, just as far as suits his critical convictions, and closes it at the words "wherein was no water." But the very next clause is, "Who brought thee forth water out of the rock of flint." Why does he omit that? Because it would not suit his purpose. Is this fair? Is it ordinary literary honesty, or common Christian integrity, to quote a text to prove one thing, when, if he would read on, it will be found to prove precisely the other thing?

He refers, at page 122, to the sacrifices that were offered in the desert. He says, "The book of Leviticus is chiefly occupied in giving directions to the priests for the proper discharge of the different duties of their office, and further directions are given in the book of Numbers. And now let us ask, for all these multifarious duties," that he quotes connected with sacrifices, "during the forty years' sojourn in the wilderness; for all the burnt-offerings, meat-offerings, peace-offerings, sin-offerings, trespass-offerings, thank-offerings, etc., of a population like that of the city of London, besides the daily and extraordinary sacrifices —how many priests were there? The answer is very simple, there were only *three*—Aaron (till his death), and his two sons, Eleazar and Ithamar. And it is laid down very solemnly in Numbers iii. 10, 'Thou shalt appoint Aaron and his sons, and they shall wait in the priest's office; and *the stranger, that cometh nigh, shall be put to death.*' So again, verse 38, 'Aaron and his sons, keeping the charge of the sanctuary, for the charge of the children of Israel; and *the stranger that cometh nigh shall be put to death.*' Yet, how was it possible, that these two or three men should have discharged all these duties for such a vast multitude? The single work of offering the double sacrifice for women after childbirth, must have utterly overpowered three priests, though engaged without cessation from morning to night. As we have seen (74), the births among two millions of people may be reckoned as, at least, 250 a day; for which, consequently, 500 sacrifices (250 burnt-offerings and 250 sin-offerings), would have had to be offered daily. Looking at the directions in Leviticus i. 4, we can scarcely allow less than *five minutes* for each sacrifice; so that these sacrifices alone, if offered separately, would have taken 2,500 minutes, or nearly 42 hours, and could not have been offered in a single day of twelve hours, though each of the three priests had been employed in one sole incessant labor of offering them, without a moment's rest or intermission. It may, perhaps, be said, that *many* such sacrifices might have been offered at the same time. This is, surely, somewhat contrary to the notion of a sacrifice, as derived from the book of Leviticus; nor is there the slightest intimation, in the whole Pentateuch, of any such heaping together of sacrifices; and it must be borne in mind, that there was but *one* altar, five cubits (about nine feet) square, Exodus xxvii. 1, at which we have already supposed all the three priests to be officiating at the same moment, actually offering, therefore, upon the altar, *three* sacrifices *at once*, of which the *burnt*-offerings would, except in the case of poor women (Leviticus xii. 8), be *lambs*, and not pigeons. But then we must ask further, where could they have obtained these 250 'turtle-doves or young pigeons' daily; that is, 90,000 annually, *in the wilderness?* There *might* be *two* offered for each birth; there *must*, according to the law, be *one*. (Lev. xii. 6, 8.) Did the people, then, carry with them *turtle-doves* and *young pigeons* out of Egypt when they fled in such haste, and so heavily laden, and as yet knew nothing of any such law? Or how could they have had them at all under Sinai? It can not be said that the laws, which require the sacrifice of such birds, were intended only to suit the circumstances of a later time, when the people should be finally settled in the land of Canaan." His argument is, therefore, that the story is incredible, and that it confutes itself. Now we turn to the literal facts of the case; and what do we find? First, the text on which the Bishop builds the conclusion that sacrifices were offered in the desert at all, is Amos v. 25; "Have ye offered unto me sacrifices and offerings in the wilderness forty years, O house of Israel?" I have turned to some of the commentators the most reliable upon this subject, and among the rest to Dr. Gill, the ablest Oriental scholar, perhaps, that ever wrote a commentary on Scripture, and he says, upon this very passage of Amos, "These sacrifices were not offered to God, but to devils—to the golden calf, and to the host of heaven. So their fathers did in the wilderness forty years, where sacrifices were omitted during that time." And again he says, on Acts vii. 42, "They offered to devils, not to God; and though *there were some few sacrifices offered up*, yet, since they were not frequently offered, nor freely, and with all the heart, and without hypocrisy, even these were looked upon by God as if they had not been offered at all." Almost all commentators admit that few, if any sacrifices, were offered in the desert, and that the sacrifices that Amos rebukes were sacrifices offered to idol gods, the golden calf, and such like. And therefore the Bishop's calculation how it was possible would be perfectly sound, if his premises were tenable; but, as the premises are false, the whole superstructure of his reasoning necessarily falls to the ground.

In a new edition of his book (and I am sorry to say it has run through two editions of some ten or twelve thousand copies in a very short period of time), he makes this remark, speaking of the command in Exodus xxxii. 27: "Thus saith the Lord God of Israel, Put every man his sword by his side, and go in and out from gate to gate throughout the camp, and slay every man his brother, and every man his companion, and every man his neighbor." The Bishop says that such a slaughter must have been something like the slaughter at Cawnpore, on a recent occasion in India. But when we come to the actual facts of the case, we find that there were twenty-two thousand Levites commanded to act. Suppose that each Levite had slain a neighbor, and a companion, and a brother, three times 22,000 would be 66,000; but the Sacred Record says that 3000 were slain; and, therefore, the Bishop's calculation, that a judicial penalty, inflicted by the Judge of all the earth, is a piece of atrocious and sanguinary butchery, is scarcely fair.

Another objection of the Bishop's is the account of the sun and moon standing still, as recorded in the

Book of Joshua. He sets it down as one of the apocryphal stories contained in the Bible ; and among other things, he shows how utterly impossible it was, according to his calculation, that any thing of the sort could have taken place. The Bishop's reasoning is contained in his introductory remarks, and at the 11th page, where he says, "Not to speak of the fact, that, if the earth's motion were suddenly stopped, a man's *feet* would be arrested, while his body was moving at the rate (on the equator) of 1,000 miles an hour," which is literal, just calculation; "or, rather, 1,000 miles a minute, since not only must the earth's diurnal rotation on its axis be stopped, but its annual motion also through space, so that every human being and animal would be dashed to pieces in a moment, and a mighty deluge overwhelm the earth;" therefore, argues the Bishop, the thing is improbable, and incredible, and absurd. He is not at all ashamed to say the Bible asserts it; but Bishop Colenso denies it, and he leaves it with Christendom to decide which is truth. In the first place, the Bishop's difficulty seems to proceed from the difficulty of conceiving or understanding the *process* by which the miracle was done. Grant the postulate Omnipotence, and the Scripture expressly says it was an Omnipotent arm that did it; what physical results and acts are impossible to Omnipotence? This alone would be a sufficient answer. But the Bishop says, No; even though Omnipotence is the agent, I must trace the process or I will not believe it. Suppose I apply the Bishop's reasoning to another miracle wrought at Cana of Galilee, where water was converted into wine. Now, if Bishop Colenso would take up that miracle, and discuss it precisely as he has discussed the miracle of the sun and moon standing still, he would talk in this way: "Water turned into wine! Where could the alcohol come from? Water is composed of oxygen and hydrogen; there is no alcohol in it. Secondly, where could the coloring matter come from? Water is limpid, whereas wine is purple or red. In the next place, where could the saccharine matter have come from? for there is saccharine matter in wine, but in water there is no sugar at all. And then where could the vegetable acid have come from? there is no vegetable acid in water, it is insipid and tasteless. Besides, wine requires fermentation; how could water have fermented without saccharine matter; and how could the fermentation have been executed in an instant? Therefore the miracle at Cana of Galilee is incredible, impossible, and, therefore, untrue." The reasoning is precisely the same. The answer to it all is, Grant Omnipotence as the power, and an arrested sun, and water turned into wine, are conceivable enough. But I will take the Bishop on his own reasoning. He says he doubts the possibility of it. I may explain that the language of Scripture is the language of the almanac. The sun rises and sets; the sun reaches his meridian; all that is popular language. We know perfectly well that the sun's rise depends upon the earth's rotation; and the earliness or lateness of the rise depends upon the earth's position in its orbit. And therefore, when it says the sun and moon stood still, it is the popular phrase, used by every astronomer in Christendom, to denote that the earth was arrested on its axis, and in its orbit also; instead of revolving on its axis, it rested; instead of marching in its orbit, it became stationary. The Bishop's argument is, If the earth, proceeding at its prodigious velocity, had been arrested suddenly, every body must have been thrown off into infinite space, and dashed to atoms. But the Bishop forgets that there are two ways of arresting a body in motion. Suppose I were traveling in a Great Western express at a rate of between fifty and sixty miles an hour; if that express were to be suddenly arrested, every traveler in it would be dashed to pieces. But the guards put on a series of breaks, and in the course of less than a quarter of a mile, it is brought to a stand-still; and you are scarcely conscious that it is arrested. Shall the guards be able to arrest a train safely, and prevent the destruction of those it carries; and shall the Great Ruler of all the earth not know how to arrest safely to its inhabitants, only a faster body — the revolution of the earth on its axis, and its movement in its own orbit? He assumes that God stopped the earth in an instant. I am taking the Bishop according to his own reasoning. God may have taken five minutes, or ten minutes, or twenty minutes to arrest it; but this we know, that it is one of the laws of dynamics that, a body moving with the highest velocity may be brought to a stop gradually as well as suddenly. And if that is true of a train, why may it not be true of the earth revolving upon its axis? The Bishop has forgotten his mathematics, as well as his religion, when he made so blundering an objection against the miracle wrought by God in the days of Joshua.

The Bishop next objects to slavery among the Jews. He is awfully shocked at the laws relating to slavery in the Old Testament Scripture. I am rather surprised that Bishop Colenso is shocked at slavery, for he must recollect that only three years ago he wrote home from Natal that he thought the Zulus ought to be permitted to have two or three wives, if they liked. How a bishop, who upholds polygamy, can so sensitively recoil from slavery, I can not determine; but it is matter of fact that some things which to our moral instincts are most objectionable, to the Bishop's moral instincts are perfectly allowable in the latitude of Natal. But we find that polygamy existed among the Jews, and we place it in the same category with slavery. And the true solution of it all is just what the great Master himself tells us, namely, that "Moses, because of the hardness of your hearts, suffered it." If you look at the Bible, you will learn from it that the human family was progressively educated, rising from a lower to a loftier form; and that what was tolerated in the lowest form was abjured and forbidden in the higher. Slavery existed among the Jews, vastly mitigated, and very different from the slavery in the South American States, for it had restrictions, and limits, and laws of the most beneficent kind. We admit, with the Bishop, it was allowed, and so was polygamy; but it was allowed because of the hardness of their hearts, and ceased as soon as they became wiser and better.

The most striking rebuke I must notice in drawing these remarks to a close is—*pro pudor!*—administered by a Jewish Rabbi to a Christian Bishop. Dr. Adler, a first-rate Hebrew scholar, as he must be, thus concludes a letter referring to Bishop Colenso:—"Had the author studied the Bible with a little greater attention, we should not have been favored with the outburst of his virtuous indignation; and the Zulu Kaffir would have been taught the true meaning of Exodus xxi. 20, 22, where Bishop Colenso would have discovered that the commandment does not refer to murder with malice prepense, but to accidental manslaughter; and that if the slave died under his master's hand it was to be avenged; and these expressions he will find explained by ancient commentators to mean, executed by the sword. In conclusion, let me ask Bishop Colenso one question. He forbids us from indulging in the imagination that God could reveal Himself to us by means of an infallible book; will he have us to believe that God could reveal Himself through a book which contains such absurdities as those that he alleges are to be found in it?"

The Bishop's difficulties arise from looking exclusively at the human side of every question; and even in this view his difficulties are not always based on sound arithmetic. He asks, How could God have done this? How could such a miracle have taken place? He forgets that all took place under a Theocracy, where God was King, and Captain, and ever-present Leader of the hosts of Israel. He leaves out God, and treats Moses as if he were the writer of a history like that of Herodotus; and even when he does this, he mistakes and blunders in his arithmetic in a way not to have been expected from one who took the high honor of a Wrangler in the University of Cambridge. But if the veracity of Moses is contingent upon, How could it be? his veracity will not be disputed only in the cases quoted by the Bishop; but we may ask, How could the granite rock have gushed forth into refreshing streams by the touch of the rod of Moses? How could a pillar of cloud, all blackness by day, have become illuminated, splendid, and glorious by night? How could the sea have been cloven in twain by the holding out of the rod of Moses, between which and the literal ocean there could be no possible connection whatever?

Bishop Colenso is the Nicodemus of the nineteenth century. His constant question is, "How can these things be?" I trust that if he has the difficulties of Nicodemus, he may obtain the grace that Nicodemus obtained too, and that the Bishop may yet live to see at once the absurdity, the contradictions, and the blunders of his book; and that we on our part may feel more profoundly that "all Scripture is given by inspiration of God," and that "Thy word, O God, is truth."

I can not help quoting and adding the following remarks by the son of the chief Rabbi of the Jews in London:—

A crop of rejoinders will, no doubt, soon spring up to refute the various arguments used by Dr. Colenso, for impugning the historical veracity of the Pentateuch. My object in writing this letter is by no means to vindicate the truth of the Bible. I consider truth to be powerful enough in itself to triumph over presumption and injustice. The Bible has, indeed, stood more powerful attacks than Dr. Colenso has been enabled to make upon it. I would simply inquire, as one of those to whom a "critical examination of the Pentateuch" is of special interest, how far the promise held out on the title-page is fulfilled in the body of the work? The author assigns as one of the reasons why it had been left to him to discover the unhistorical character of the Pentateuch, the little progress which Biblical studies have as yet made among the English clergy, and the neglect of the study of the Hebrew language (p. 21). Dr. Colenso is not, I fear, much in advance of his brethren. In sect. 53, he says that Lev. xxiii. 40 — "Ye shall take you the boughs," etc.—contains the description of the way in which the booths to be used during the Feast of Tabernacles were to be made!—a mistake which may be overlooked if made by the brilliant author of "Coningsby," but it is unpardonable in one who is an eminent divine, and is anxious to be considered a learned critic. A Jewish child would set the Bishop right on this point, and inform him that the four vegetable productions were to be taken into the temple "to rejoice before the Lord seven days," and are in no way connected with the booths.

We can easily see, however, why he has fallen into this egregious error. The author does not seem to have consulted the original; he suffers himself to be bound in the trammels of the authorized version, and servilely copies its mistranslations.

And further, throughout the criticism, the author wholly ignores the labors of the Jewish commentators in the same field. He devotes so much space (chaps. ii. and iii.) to show that the clumsy devices of Kurtz and Hengstenberg for reconciling the difficulty about the family of Judah are untenable, but does not allude to the simple solution suggested by the critical Ibn Ezra, that the idiom used need not be taken literally, but that the event recorded in that chapter may have taken place many years before (just as in Deut. x. 8).

It is indeed a strange occurrence to find the Jew, in the nineteenth century, more zealous for the integrity of God's Holy Word than the Bishop of Natal.

CHAPTER V.

THE PASSOVER AND ITS SIGNIFICANCE.

EXODUS XII. 1–13.

"AND the Lord spake unto Moses and Aaron in the land of Egypt, saying, This month shall be unto you the beginning of months: it shall be the first month of the year to you. Speak ye unto all the congregation of Israel, saying, In the tenth day of this month they shall take to them every man a lamb, according to the house of their fathers, a lamb for an house: and if the household be too little for the lamb, let him and his neighbor next unto his house take it according to the number of the souls; every man according to his eating shall make your count for the lamb. Your lamb shall be without blemish, a male of the first year: ye shall take it out from the sheep, or from the goats: and ye shall keep it up until the fourteenth day of the same month; and the whole assembly of the congregation of Israel shall kill it in the evening. And they shall take of the blood, and strike it on the two side posts and on the upper door post of the houses, wherein they shall eat it. And they shall eat the flesh in that night, roast with fire, and unleavened bread; and with bitter herbs they shall eat it. Eat not of it raw, nor sodden at all with water, but roast with fire; his head with his legs, and with the purtenance thereof. And ye shall let nothing of it remain until the morning; and that which remaineth of it until the morning ye shall burn with fire. And thus shall ye eat it; with your loins girded, your shoes on your feet, and your staff in your hand; and ye shall eat it in haste: it is the Lord's passover. For I will pass through the land of Egypt this night, and will smite all the firstborn in the land of Egypt, both man and beast;

and against all the gods of Egypt I will execute judgment: I am the Lord. And the blood shall be to you for a token upon the houses where ye are: and when I see the blood, I will pass over you, and the plague shall not be upon you to destroy you, when I smite the land of Egypt."

It is strange that the most determined and the most unjustifiable assault by the Bishop of Natal on the institutions and the facts of the ancient economy has been made on this most beautiful, most suggestive, and evangelical institution. I have already discussed various details of arithmetical and mathematical objections laid against certain portions of Scripture, and having got rid of these, we now come into the open sea, for the discussion of great and suggestive truths, that, like the sun in the firmament, prove themselves simply by their shining. God gives command, and says, "I will pass through the land of Egypt this night." (Exodus xii. 12.) The Bishop argues that the instruction was given to the Israelites to select a lamb that very night, to kill that lamb, to sprinkle the door-posts, and to be off in that very morning as fast as their feet could carry them. He argues, mathematically as before, but absurdly as usual, that this was incredible and impossible. But he never can have read the chapter fairly, or at least with his mind awake to the suggestive points that it contains; for I should draw an inference just the reverse of what he draws. He says, the command was given and the lamb slain that same night. The strict law of the institution is contained in the third verse: "In the tenth day of this month they shall take to them every man a lamb." They were to keep it till the fourteenth day of the month, and on the fourteenth day of the month they were to slay it. But what does that imply? That the selection of the lamb was made upon the tenth day; that it was kept in silence for examination four days; that on the fourteenth day, between the evenings, or between three and six o'clock in the afternoon, it was slain. When God refers to "this night," He means the night on which the lamb was slain; "I will pass through Egypt." He does not teach that the lamb was both selected and slain that same night, on which God passed in judgment through Egypt; on the contrary, He says expressly it was to be selected on the tenth, it was to be slain upon the fourteenth; and on this very night, that is, the fourteenth, "I will pass through the land of Egypt, and will execute judgment upon the firstborn of Egypt," "from the firstborn of Pharaoh that sitteth upon his throne, even unto the firstborn of the maid-servant that is behind the mill." How, therefore, any one reading this can have made so gross and palpable a mistake, I can not possibly conceive; but it is gratifying to know that the detection of the mistake is so obvious, and the refutation of the seeming impossibility so easy.

The next objection of the Bishop which I will notice, before I enter upon the meaning, the magnificent meaning of this institution, is, How was it possible that in the land of Egypt they could have got what was actually requisite—lambs at all equal in number to the houses of Israel? How could they have found pasture for two million sheep, the minimum number requisite to supply so many lambs to the vast multitude, for passover sacrifices on that memorable night? This is the question that he asks, and to which his answer is, It was impossible. And in order to show that it was impossible, the Bishop says, that in Natal, where he had been accustomed to work, one sheep only could be fed upon one acre; and he also calculates the relative sizes of Egypt, and Goshen, and Natal; and his inference is, that it is impossible that any thing like a million, much less two million sheep, could have been fed upon all the pastures of the land of Egypt; and therefore his argument is, there could not have been found as many lambs as were requisite—a lamb for a house—to celebrate the passover on that memorable night when the angel of the Lord passed through, and slew the first-born of Egypt. The answer that we give is—first, the sacred narrative asserts that the requisite number was found; secondly, Natal is not Egypt, and he would require to show that the cases were perfectly parallel before the one could be a perfect illustration of the other; and that if the Bishop, instead of looking to Natal to ascertain how many sheep could be fed upon an acre, had only retained some reminiscences of his native land, he would have found the following fact, which has been quoted by the Rev. Mr. M'Caul, from "Fullarton's Gazetteer," published in Edinburgh in 1856, under the heading "Dorset, the county of Dorset." The statement there is as follows:—"Through the central parts of the county of Dorset runs a ridge of chalk hills, declining on the south side into downs and valleys, which abound in a short, sweet herbage, nourishing from 800,000 to 1,000,000 sheep." Now, if one county in England, or rather a section of a county of England, can nourish a million sheep (and this is a matter of statistics), the Bishop surely might have had the common sense to infer that the land of Goshen, rich in the richest pasture, could have nourished, not two millions—which he says it never could have nourished—but five or six million sheep; taking the pasture of the county of Dorset as the guiding element in our calculation. Therefore the arguments of the Bishop do not hold water, the illustrations he employs fail, and the irresistible fact stands out before us, that God's Word, whether you appeal to the facts of history, or to the phenomena of nature, or to the earth with its pastures, justifies itself, and vindicates its author God, its inspiration truth, and its end evermore the happiness of mankind and the glory of God!

But without dwelling more upon these points, which are really not the most weighty and conclusive reasons of all, we will turn to the marvelous coïncidence between the type, or the passover-lamb, and the Antitype, or Christ crucified; and we shall see that it is impossible to come to any other conclusion than that the one was a Divine institution, pre-figurative and pre-significant of the other. Let us study a portion of the language that expresses it. We have seen it in the 12th of Exodus, we find it also alluded to in the 13th; also in Deuteronomy xvi.; also in Isaiah liii. Read carefully, at your leisure, the 53d of Isaiah, and what will be your inference? That the whole language is paschal language, that every allusion in it indicates the Paschal Lamb to be the event to which it refers, "He is brought as a lamb to the slaughter, and as a sheep before her shearers is dumb, so He openeth not His mouth." Turn again to the institution of the Lord's Supper, in the 26th chapter of the Gospel of St. Matthew, and see what is said there; we read: "Now the first day of the feast of unleavened bread the disciples came to Jesus, saying unto Him, Where wilt thou that we prepare for thee to eat the passover?" The disciples believed in the institution, and in its obligation from year to year. But what did Jesus say? Did He say, The passover is a myth — it was a delusion that Moses was led into, or that the Jews adopted — it is not a fact; or, in the language of the Bishop of Natal, It is unhistorical and untrue? If the Saviour had so said, the argument would be finished. But what does He say? Let us read; "Go into the city to such a man, and say unto him, The Master saith, My time is at hand; I will keep the passover at thy house with my disciples." That implies that the Saviour believed in the passover as an ancient Levitical institution. Well, we read next: "And the disciples did as Jesus had appointed them; and they made ready the passover." Can we suppose that our blessed Lord celebrated a myth, that He justified the observance of a mere vague, unfounded tradition; or that the Lord's Supper grew out of a romance, a falsehood, a lie? It is impossible. Yet that is the alternative we are driven to, if the passover was not an historical fact, was not an institution that had Divine sanction, and was not, and could not, as Dr. Colenso says, have been observed by the ancient Jews. If we turn to the 6th of John, we shall understand its meaning most easily by bearing in mind the passover throughout. For instance, "Jesus said unto them, I am the bread of life." And again, He says, lower down in the chapter, at the 51st verse, "I am the living bread which came down from heaven: if any man eat of this bread, he shall live forever: and the bread that I will give is my flesh, which I will give for the life of the world. The Jews therefore strove among themselves, saying, How can this man give us his flesh to eat? Then Jesus said unto them, Verily, verily, I say unto you, Except ye eat the flesh of the Son of man, and drink his blood, ye have no life in you." This seems very violent language, unless there be some underlying allusion to justify and bear it out. But we find that after the lamb was slain in the ancient usage of Israel, its flesh was eaten to denote the interest of the people in it; and therefore the language of Jesus, "Except ye eat my flesh, and drink my blood," means, that I am the Lamb about to be offered up a sacrifice, and that your life in this world, your hopes for the next, your strength, your security, your peace, are all derived from your feeding on me and living by me; so that the life that you live you live by the faith of the Son of God, who loved you and gave Himself for you. There is other language equally allusive. When Jesus appeared, what did John the Baptist say? "Behold the Lamb of God, which taketh away the sin of the world." What was that? Paschal or passover language; as if he said to them: "The passover lamb, selected on the tenth and slain on the fourteenth, is gone; it is a shadow that has now passed away; behold the Lamb — the true passover Lamb — that taketh away the sin of the world." Again, we read in Acts viii. 32, referring to Isaiah liii.: "He was led as a sheep to the slaughter; and like a lamb dumb before his shearers, so opened He not His mouth." Again, we read in 1 Cor. v. 7: "Christ our passover is sacrificed for us; therefore let us keep the feast, not with old leaven, neither with the leaven of malice and wickedness, but with the unleavened bread of sincerity and truth." That this passover was a fact, is obvious from the language that is used even in the songs of heaven; for we read in the book of Revelation, at the fifth chapter: "And when He had taken the book, the four living creatures and four and twenty elders fell down before the Lamb, having every one of them harps, and golden vials full of odors, which are the prayers of saints. And they sung a new song, saying, Thou art worthy to take the book, and to open the seals thereof: for thou wast slain," ("and thou shalt slay it between the evenings,") "and hast redeemed us to God by thy *blood* out of every kindred, and tongue, and people, and nation; and hast made us unto our God kings and priests: and we shall reign on the earth. And I beheld, and I heard the voice of many angels round about the throne and the beasts and the elders: and the number of them was ten thousand times ten thousand, and thousands of thousands; saying with a loud voice, Worthy is the Lamb that was *slain* to receive power, and riches, and wisdom, and strength, and honor, and glory, and blessing. And every creature which is in heaven, and on the earth, and under the earth, and such as are in the sea, and all that are in them, heard I saying, Blessing, and honor, and glory, and power, be unto Him that sitteth upon the throne, and unto the Lamb for ever and ever." Put all these allusions together, and take the language of Peter: "Ye were not redeemed with silver and gold, but with the precious blood of Christ, as of a lamb without blemish and without spot;" "without blemish"—mark that word: "A lamb of the flock, a male without blemish." And what must be the inference? That the whole New Testament Scripture regards the passover sacrifice as the most expressive illustration of Christ our Passover, slain for us; and that much of the language of the New Testament is inexplicable unless we assume that the passover was a fact; and that what we read in the 12th of Exodus was the ritual and the rubric for the observance of that ancient institution ordained by God Himself.

Why do I state these things? Not because Christians doubt, but because skeptics, or those of a skeptical turn of mind, are very apt to raise the superstructure of grand conclusions upon vague and unfounded misinterpretations of plain and obvious passages in the Word of God. Nothing can be plainer than the evidence that the passover was instituted by God; that it was observed on that memorable night ever to be remembered; and that lambs sufficient were provided for it. And as to the difficulties which the Bishop unhappily conjures up, they are difficulties that beset every thing upon earth. We breathe difficulties; we are surrounded by difficulties. How can I explain the process by which my mind, an immaterial force, acts upon my body, a material subject? How can I explain Omnipresence, or Omnipotence, or the existence of Deity, or my own existence, or a thousand things? The difficulties that beset a theme are reasons for its study, not valid objections to its truth.

Having disposed of the Bishop's difficulties, I would now try to feed the flock with the great truths that are contained in this passage. First, the origin of the institution was Israel's deliverance. The iron had pierced their souls; their groans and cries rose up to heaven for liberty. They felt Egypt was not their home; its flesh-pots could not be their bread; its air could not be their life. God resolved, therefore, in the exercise of mercy upon them, but in the infliction of terrible judgments upon Pharaoh, to emancipate them with a high hand and with an outstretched arm. The process that He adopted we read in the 12th chapter of Exodus. What is the first lesson it there teaches? First, all blessings that ever have been tasted by the ancient church, all the mercies that can possibly be received or enjoyed by us, are intimately associated with sacrifice. Israel never had a blessing till it was sprinkled with atoning blood; we never can have a mercy, from a crumb of bread to a crown of glory, from the air we breathe to the sunshine of heaven we hope to enjoy, unless sprinkled by atoning blood. There is not a shower on the field, nor a spring in the valley, nor a loaf upon your table, nor a cup of water in your hand, nor a happy beat in your heart, nor a bright fire on your hearth, that is not associated with and dependent on that cross which was raised on Calvary—that sacrifice "Christ our passover sacrificed for us." There is not a rest that you enjoy in the present, there is not a blessed hope that you cherish, there is not a truth revealed in the Bible, there is not a ray of sunshine that descends from the sanctuary above, that is not intimately and inseparably connected with Christ and with

Him crucified. There center all our best and our brightest hopes; there die and disappear our worst and our most perplexing fears; there is seen the price of the least and the loftiest blessing that you, and your children, and your children's children, ever enjoyed or can enjoy upon earth. The cross lies broad, and deep, and palpable to a Christian heart upon all earth's blessings, upon all heaven's joys; and by that cross alone can the greatest saint—and, thank God, may the greatest sinner—climb to the heights of glory. Such is the first lesson.

The second lesson I would learn from this institution is, the lamb selected for the sacrifice was required to be—and this is laid down as an essential part of the institution—without blemish, or a lamb without spot. Let us mark the coïncidence between the institution that has passed away, and the blessed Saviour it foreshadowed, who remains; and see if the coïncidence between them is not evidence that the one was a fact, and that the other is its solution and its end. The Saviour is declared by the apostle Peter to have been a Lamb without blemish or without spot; He is declared to have been "that holy thing that shall be born of thee." It is said of Him again, "In Him was no sin." *On* Him was the mountain load of a world's sin; *in* Him was no sin at all. Our sins were *on* Him, not *in* Him, therefore He was slain; and, blessed be God, His righteousness is *on* us, not *in* us, therefore we are justified and accepted of Him from everlasting to everlasting. Our sins lay heavy upon Him, but not one taint or touch of them was in that holy, holy, holy heart of His; His righteousness never can be *in* us, but it is imputed *to* us; and just as that Saviour, when He died upon the cross, was infinitely innocent, so when you and I shall stand on the margin of heaven, we shall be then and there miserable sinners, but accepted through the perfect righteousness of Him, Christ our Passover, sacrificed for us. He was the innocent when He died; we shall be the guilty when we are justified. Our sins on Him, not in Him, dragged Him to the accursed tree; His righteousness on us, with nothing in us, shall entitle us to the heights of heaven, and to everlasting blessedness and joy!

The lamb, the passover lamb, was set apart on the tenth day, and it was killed on the fourteenth day, between the evenings; that is, from three to six o'clock in the evening. Here, notice again the coïncidence—and the coïncidence, while instructive to us as Christians, is confirmatory of what Moses has recorded respecting that institution. The lamb, set apart four days, by its silence eloquently impressed upon Israel the necessity for this sacrifice. The Saviour set apart from His baptism by the Holy Ghost, when the Holy Ghost descended upon Him, till He died, nearly four years—a day for a year being the ordinary rule in prophecy; and during these four years, He taught His great lessons, preached His blessed sermons, spake in beautiful and suggestive parables, performed stupendous miracles, and gave the whole land lessons that live along the ages, and are the sunshine, and the hope, and the inspiration of increasing thousands of mankind. And during all these four years in which the Saviour was set apart, Satan searched Him, and had nothing to say against Him; Pilate examined Him, and he was constrained to say, "I find no fault in him;" officers, and soldiers, and constables, sent to take Him, came back and said, "Never man spake like this man." Justified by heaven, acquitted by earth, searched by Satan, pronounced faultless in echoes that reverberated through the whole universe, He died, the infinitely innocent One, in the room and stead of us, the guilty and the fallen children of Adam.

We are told that the passover, after its first institution and celebration in the land of Egypt, must ever afterwards be celebrated in Jerusalem. So Christ, our Passover, died not in Bethlehem, not in Jericho, not in imperial Rome, not in æsthetic and cultivated Athens, but in Jerusalem our Passover was sacrificed for us. The coïncidence, therefore, here, too, is complete; and such coïncidences are arguments. If you find a lock — one of Bramah's, or Chubb's, or Hobbs' locks — of excessively intricate structure, and with wards the most perplexing, and you find a key that fits the wards and opens the lock, you infer that the key was meant for the lock, and the lock was meant for the key. There are between Christ our Passover and the Jewish passover such coïncidences, such a perfect adaptation of the one to the other that the inference of every man — excepting, of course, the Bishop of Natal — must be that the one was designed to prefigure the other; and that Christ, our Passover, is the substitute now for the great historic fact of the passover lamb slain on that memorable night of the march of Israel from the thralldom and the bondage of Egypt.

I pass on to another truth, and a most suggestive and precious one it is for us. After the lamb was slain and offered up, its blood was caught, we are told, in a basin, a bunch of hyssop was dipped into the basin, and the blood was sprinkled on the door-post and the lintel of the house in which the lamb was slain. Here we have the proof that the atonement made by the sacrifice of that lamb was the safety of the children of Israel. When the angel of death swept on strong pinion through the length and breadth of Egypt, on that memorable and awful night, and when he wished to ascertain where he should strike and where he should spare, what guided him? He did not ask what were the virtues of the father of the household within, that he might spare on account of them; nor what were the sins of the family within the house, that he might strike there. These were inquiries he did not institute. The safety of the house was not the virtue of its inmates, not the goodness of the father, nor the love of the mother, nor the obedience of the children —

virtues of course beautiful in their place; the safety of each house in that dark night, in the midst of Egypt, was something outside, not any thing within; it was the blood sprinkled on the lintel and door-posts of the house. The angel's mission was to strike — not where sin had been perpetrated within, but — where there was no blood upon the lintel; and the command to the angel was to spare—not where there were virtues in the lives of the inmates of the house, but—where there was blood sprinkled visibly upon the lintel and the door-posts of the house. Magnificent, glorious truth! your safety is not the virtues you have practiced, nor the graces that adorn you, nor the unimpeachable spotlessness of all your antecedents combined — things in their place and of themselves dutiful and beautiful before God and before mankind; your safety, your only safety, is in blood shed for you, not in any thing done by you. Your safety in the hour of death, your acquittal at the judgment throne, your right to everlasting glory, the reason of your exemption from all the curses that are written in this law, is nothing done in you, nothing suffered by you, nothing paid by you; but wholly, solely, perfectly, and completely, the blood that has been shed by Christ our Passover, sacrificed for us. And if that blood be sprinkled upon you; if you have washed your robes, to use the language of the Apocalypse, and made them white in the blood of the Lamb; neither sin, nor Satan, nor life, nor death, nor angels, nor principalities, nor powers, nor height, nor depth, nor any other creature, shall be able to separate you from the love of God that is in Jesus Christ our Lord. "The blood of Jesus Christ His Son cleanseth from all sin." "We have remission by His blood, even the forgiveness of sins." Do you believe that? Have you trust in that? Can you lay the stress of your everlasting prospects upon this, that nothing done by you, nothing done in you, nothing pledged, promised, or paid by any one on earth, but that blood that has been shed for you—can you say this is enough? Let the Bishop of Natal quibble; let him conjure up difficulties like specters from the distant and the gloomy past; but let the humblest Christian say, and be assured while he says it, that it will stand him in stead in that day, "I know, whatever he knows, I know in whom I have believed, and that Christ is able to keep what I have committed to Him against that day, and to present me faultless before His presence in glory with exceeding joy."

Here, then, is the great truth of Christ our Passover, sacrificed for us. What a pity that a Christian minister should give up so splendid a lesson in deference to perplexing quibbles and difficulties, which in themselves are not founded in fact, and which, if we could not solve them, are not sufficient to disprove a plain historical institution, interwoven, like woof and warp, with the whole texture of the Bible and of Christianity.

I take another lesson from this most precious institution. The lamb was not only slain a sacrifice, and its blood the shelter of every house—just as Christ has been slain, not a martyr, not a victim, but a sacrifice, and His blood the shelter of every heart—but, as we read of that institution, after the lamb was slain, and its blood had been the shelter, its flesh was roasted, and was eaten by the household assembled that memorable night beneath the shadow of the blood-protected roof.

But, how do we explain this in reference to the great Antitype? It is here we have the explanation:—"Except ye eat the flesh and drink the blood of the Son of man, ye have no life in you." It was literally applied to the Jew; you must kill the lamb, you must shed its blood, that blood must be your protection; but except you eat its flesh, as God has instituted, you can not have the enjoyment of all the fruits and the benefits of that Divine institution. But how can this be applied to us? I answer, a Christian does not feed upon Christ's righteousness, or upon Christ's pardon, but on Christ, to use the Scripture language; he eats the flesh, he drinks the blood of the Son of man, but not at the communion-table, where we materially eat bread and drink wine; but really and truly, because spiritually, by faith, throughout his whole life and conduct, from time to eternity. Let me explain it. If I were to tell you that a tree feeds upon air, and light, and sunshine, you would not imagine that I meant to convey that a tree masticates the air, and the light, and the sunshine, as you and I eat food. All that the phrase would convey to you, or to any intelligent man, would be, that the nature of a tree is such that by its structure it absorbs the light, and the air, and the sunshine; and it grows in size and strength, and derives nutriment by doing so. In the same manner when we say, a Christian eats the flesh and drinks the blood of the Son of man, we do not mean that he literally masticates these, which is monstrous and absurd; but that just as the tree feeds upon light, and sunshine, and air, so the Christian, according to the very nature of his soul, feeds upon what Christ is, is nourished and strengthened by the knowledge of what Christ has done, and appropriates Christ, as the tree appropriates air, and light, and sunshine, that which is the nutriment of his soul, the joy of his spirit, and the hope of his heart, through everlasting ages. The phrase is purely figurative, and is meant to convey, not that a Christian literally eats flesh and drinks blood at the Lord's table, which would be a monstrous carnal delusion; but that by the very nature of his soul, believing on and looking to the Lord Jesus Christ, he appropriates from Him that finished righteousness, which is his trust, that atoning efficacy in His death which is his pardon, that peace which he needs amidst the world's troubles, and that hope which stretches into everlasting ages. And thus a Christian can say literally, "I live, yet not I, but Christ liveth in me; and the life that I live I live through the power and faith of the Son of God, who loved me and gave Himself for me!" Here, then, you have the passover Lamb partaken of.

Let me notice, in the next place, that the safety of the household, as I have shown you, was derived wholly from the blood sprinkled on the threshold; but the inner comfort of the Israelite, notwithstanding this, may not have been great. I can conceive that some mother clasped more tightly in her arms her first-born, when she heard the beat of the angel's wings as he swept through every street in broad Egypt, and as she listened to the wail that rose from the next door, where father and mother gazed upon their first-born stricken dead by the angel's breath; that she trembled and feared, while her heart beat violently, dreading lest the next stroke should lay her first-born pale and cold beside her; and she clasped it to her bosom only the more ardently as she thought of and feared the death that might soon overtake it. But what did her husband say to her? He said, "You are afraid, you are troubled; you love your child, you clasp and hold it fast, and you do well; but your safety is not here, but there — the blood sprinkled on the lintel; and your comfort must be there also; and you may have perfect peace, not because you are excellent, but because the blood of the lamb has been sprinkled upon the door-post." The inmate of the blood-besprinkled house, by doubts and fears, natural and to be expected, imperiled her comfort; but these doubts and fears did not in the least shake her indestructible safety before heaven and before earth. Many true Christians who approach the Lord's table come with doubts,—doubts that they can not keep down, fears that thrust up like bubbles from the depths of a deep sea, anxieties that they would crush, but can not; and sometimes they say to themselves, "Well, really, I begin almost to doubt that I am a Christian at all." This is not only likely, but common. But what is to be your peace? Whence your comfort? Not wrestling with these doubts, and difficulties, and perplexities, that rise from the swamps of the old Adam who still clings to you, and clasps you round. Your sense of peace, your encouragement, your joy, must be the blood that was shed for you, and not the good things and the grand things that have been done by you. Your right and title to come to the Lord's table, is not your virtues, nor your charities, nor your goodness, nor any thing in you, nor any thing done by you; but what Christ has suffered for you, or the blood upon the lintel and the door-posts of your heart. We shall never know what the safety, and the peace, and the happiness, and the joy of a Christian are, till we learn never by introspective looks to try to pump out peace and happiness from our own empty hearts; but by looking outside to see what was done for us 1830 years ago; and, then, justified by faith, we shall have peace with God through Jesus Christ our Lord. Oh! who, who would willingly give up so precious a truth, so suggestive a lesson, so blessed a gospel as the gospel of the passover, Christ our Passover, sacrificed for us!

One thought more, and I have done. It is this:—There were two things in the passover. First, the father had to take a lamb, and he had to shed its blood—a painful act to a sensitive mind. No man can see an animal die without feeling pain; and if we are the cause of that pain, we must be the more grieved and vexed. This was the *painful* part. But after the lamb was slain, and during successive ages, there followed what was the *pleasant* part—namely, the family gathered round, ate the roasted flesh, with bitter herbs, and a cup of wine; that was the *pleasant*, or the joyous part. In ancient Egypt, on that memorable night, and during after ages, year by year, the poor Jew had to do the painful part, which was to kill the lamb, as well as to enjoy the pleasant part, which was to drink the wine and eat the flesh. But in Christendom, magnificent bequest, glorious heritage! Jesus took to Himself *all the painful* part, and finished it; and He has bequeathed to us all the *pleasant part*, the feast that succeeds the sacrifice. Our passover was finished 1830 years ago; but our feast upon the passover is continued year by year, till Christ return crowned with many crowns.

CHAPTER VI.

THE EXODUS.

I HAVE investigated the Bishop's objections to the fact of the passover. Contrary to the notion of this prelate, who has written with great subtlety, but with great rashness upon these acts of ancient history, I have shown that the passover is an historic fact; that no man reading the Scriptures with an impartial and unprejudiced mind can come logically or reasonably to any other conclusion than that the passover was neither a myth nor a Jewish tradition, but an institution based on fact, and perpetuated by the Divine command, till, having fulfilled its purpose, like the morning twilight, it was resolved into the sunshine that brightens more and more into the noon of everlasting day. How the Bishop of Natal can maintain what he has stated upon this subject, it is hard to say. Our blessed Lord tells His disciples, "Go and find a place where I may eat the passover." Can it be said, or will any man maintain, that the Saviour accepted a tradition, a myth, a usage unhistorical and unreal, and thus celebrated an ancient sham as His farewell to an economy that had served its object and was about to pass away? Or can the apostle

Paul have supposed that he was dealing with and sanctioning a mere myth when he said, "Christ our passover is sacrificed for us"? But apart altogether from these direct Scriptural allusions to it, there is the undeniable fact, that the passover perfectly fits the atonement of Christ, and just as the key fits the wards of Bramah's intricate lock, and proves that it was made for the lock, so the harmony between the passover that has ceased and the atonement that endures is so perfect, in its most minute details, that it is impossible to escape the conclusion that God instituted the one to set forth and foreshadow the other.

I pass on to another inquiry, to the results of which, as in all previous investigations, the Bishop objects in the strongest terms. He maintains that the whole story of the Exodus and journey through the desert is incredible, or, to say the least, improbable. This is really monstrous—so much so, that to Christian minds the refutation of it must appear unnecessary; but to young men who have read little on this once more rising controversy, these expositions must be useful. It is not for the sake of the Bishop of Natal that I would dispose of his difficulties, but because it gives an opportunity of replying to objections, obsolete and old, long and constantly urged. The truth is, the Bishop's objections are old ghosts conjured up by his episcopal incantation, clothed in the raiment of the nineteenth century, and paraded upon the stage of the world as if he had excavated marvels and made brilliant discoveries in virgin soil.

The Bishop asserts very strongly that it is altogether incredible, at all events highly improbable, that the Israelites spent so many years in the desert, and found in that wild and bleak wilderness food for themselves, and pasture for their cattle. He says, under chapter xii., "The story,"—as he phrases it in his contemptuous treatment of Scripture, which to Christian minds is most distressing—"represents them as possessing these flocks and herds during the whole of the forty years which they spent in the wilderness. It can not be pretended that the state of the country through which they traveled has undergone any material change from that time to this. It is described as being then what it is now, a 'desert land,' a 'waste, howling wilderness,' Deuteronomy xxxii. 10. 'Why have ye brought the congregation of Jehovah into this wilderness, that we and our cattle should die there? And wherefore have ye made us to come up out of Egypt, to bring us unto this evil place? It is no place of seed, or of figs, or of vines, or of pomegranates; *neither is there any water to drink!*'" Numbers xx. 4, 5. Now, says the Bishop, that being the state of the desert, how can we, as rational men, suppose that two millions of people, with cattle and sheep, and flocks of immense extent, lived in a desert where there was no water,—a waste, howling wilderness—with nothing sufficient to supply their every-day wants and necessities? The great answer, whatever improbability appears to his mind, is, God so records it. But if the Bishop had read the picture of the waste, howling wilderness from beginning to end, or rather, if he had not picked out the points that suited his purpose, and ignored and unpardonably passed over the intimations that destroy that purpose, he would have come to a very different but just conclusion. It is quite true that the inspired penman says, "He found him in a desert land, and in the waste howling wilderness;" just as the Bishop quotes it. But what does the sacred penman add? "He made him to ride on the high places of the earth, that he might eat the increase of the fields; and he made him to suck honey out of the rock, and oil out of the flinty rock; butter of kine, and milk of sheep, with fat of lambs, and rams of the breed of Bashan, and goats, with the fat of kidneys of wheat; and thou didst drink the pure blood of the grape." Let the Bishop account for the fact as he likes; it is nevertheless stated in the one clause it was a waste, howling wilderness, it was a desert; but in the next, that God there gave them milk, and oil, and honey, and bread in inexhaustible abundance. Why has the Bishop passed by these modifying statements? He is partial, querulous, blind. He reads the story of the exode as he reads the history of Herodotus, Tacitus, or Cæsar, only not so carefully. He forgets that the whole of Israel's history is upon a loftier plane, a higher level, and amid a celestial light. God in the midst of them, turning rock into water, and showers into bread, is as real a fact as their march through the desert, or their passage through the cloven billows of the Red Sea. I would specially urge on every Christian, that it be borne in mind, in reading the Scriptures, that it is the Word of God which records the work of God; and the work of God would not be credible were it not written in the Word of God, which is avowedly inspired. God was as much in the desert through which the Israelites passed as He was at the foundation of the world, the creation of the stars, and the arrangement of the whole universe. It is a sad tendency which in the present day pervades our literature to a very deplorable extent, the tendency to find a world without a Maker: life without a providence: the Bible without inspiration, and its history without God. With the settled belief that Deity was visibly and sensibly present, and imminent in all the history of Israel, its most sublime acts become not only credible but reasonable. God was in the pillar of cloud, God was by the Red Sea, God was in Egypt, God was in every chapter of that strange history. The history of the Exodus is simply lifting up a corner of the curtain, and letting us see the facts that transpire on earth, and the phenomena that flash through the sky as the mere outward and visible exponents of Him whose finger is on the springs of the universe, and whose footprints are on the sands of the desert.

But there is one glaring blunder here, in relation to this passage, perfectly unpardonable on the part of the Bishop — I mean unpardonable in him as a critic and interpreter of Scripture. Speaking from Numbers xx. 4, 5, he says: "From this passage it appears also that the water from the rock did *not* follow them, as some have supposed." He quotes the words of the murmurers, let it be observed — "Neither is there any water to drink;" and then he says: "From this passage it is plain that the water from the rock did not follow the Israelites, as some have supposed." I will not charge the Bishop with being intentionally dishonest. I think all controversy that imputes motives, or that supposes or assumes that one of the controversialists is capable of deliberately misrepresenting, is to be deprecated; yet it is to me most extraordinary that the Bishop should make an assertion from the 20th chapter of the book of Numbers, that the water from the rock did not follow them. The words in Numbers xx. 5, are: "It is no place of seed, or of figs, or of vines, or of pomegranates; neither is there any water to drink." That was what the Israelites complained of. The Bishop says: "From this passage it appears also that the water from the rock did *not* follow them, as some have supposed." He seems not to have read the chapter, for it was *after* the Israelites murmured that "there was no water," that God commanded Moses to strike the rock, and the waters gushed forth. The Bishop assumes that the water from the rock was not following them, because they complained there was no water; whereas their complaint of no water was previous to the striking of the rock, and was the occasion of its being struck, in order to yield the water, of the want of which they so bitterly complained. Let us read it, because it shows the Bishop to be rash, and reckless, and unreliable. I will venture to say that one of our Sunday-school children would have exposed the Bishop's error here most triumphantly. I fear he needs to go to school to learn. Sunday-school children do not perpetrate blunders so palpably unhistorical and unworthy. In the 20th chapter of the book of Numbers we read at the second verse the words of the complaint: "And there was no water for the congregation: and they gathered themselves together against Moses and against Aaron. And the people chode with Moses, and spake, saying, Would God that we had died when our brethren died before the Lord! And why have ye brought up the congregation of the Lord into this wilderness, that we and our cattle should die there? And wherefore have ye made us to come up out of Egypt, to bring us in unto this evil place?" Now, as the Bishop quotes, "It is no place of seed, or of figs, or of vines, or of pomegranates; neither is there any water to drink." "Wherefore," says the Bishop, "the water from the rock did not follow them through the desert." Well, read on. "And Moses and Aaron went from the presence of the assembly unto the door of the tabernacle of the congregation, and they fell upon their faces: and the glory of the Lord appeared unto them. And the Lord spake unto Moses, saying, Take the rod, and gather thou the assembly together, thou, and Aaron thy brother, and speak ye unto the rock before their eyes; and it shall give forth his water, and thou shalt bring forth to them water out of the rock: so thou shalt give the congregation and their beasts drink." The Bishop quotes the complaint, "there was no water;" the rock therefore evidently did not follow them; it is all a myth — a fabulous legend — incredible and subversive of the pretensions of the Pentateuch. The historic statement of Moses clearly demonstrates that there was plenty of food for man, and grass for the cattle, and abundance of water to drink. The Bishop of Natal has now time to read the chapter. If he will do so, he may discover that Dr. Colenso is still wrong, and Moses still right. Another edition of his work is about to come out. I believe it has already reached nearly twenty thousand. I hope the powerful battery that has been opened upon his absurdities, his inaccuracies, his misquotations, and his illogical fallacies, will lead him, through God's grace, to correct what he has written, and to repent of the shock he has so unwarrantably communicated to thousands in Christendom.

But he follows up his attack still farther, and quotes a long and valuable passage from Canon Stanley, a man of piety and learning — we hope only slightly, if actually, tinged with the characteristic views of what is called the broad school of theology. The Bishop says the whole peninsula of Sinai—of which you will find in Bagster's Bible some admirable maps; in which maps you may easily trace the route of the Israelites — a route popularly and usually assumed to have been along the peninsula of Sinai, crossing the Red Sea at Suez, moving along the peninsula toward the Gulf of Elan, and thence northward to Canaan or Palestine. The Bishop quotes testimony from Canon Stanley, to the effect that the whole of that peninsula is so bleak, that it is utterly impossible — though Moses asserts it, if Moses ever was a living person — to suppose that cattle and sheep could have had herbage to eat, or could have found water to drink. Canon Stanley says: "The wind drove us to shore — the shore of Arabia and Asia. We landed in a driving sand-storm, and reached this place, Ayun-Musa, the Wells of Moses. It is a strange spot, this plot of tamarisks, with its seventeen wells, *literally an island in the desert*, and now used as the Richmond of Suez — a comparison which chiefly serves to show what a place Suez itself must be. Behind that African range lay Egypt, with all its wonders — the green fields of the Nile, the immense cities, the greatest monuments of human power and wisdom. *On this Asiatic side begins immediately a wide circle of level desert, stone, and sand*, free as air, but with no trace of human habitation or art, where they might wander, as far as they saw, for ever and ever. And between the two rolled the deep waters of the Red Sea, rising and falling with the tides, which, except on its shores, none of them could have seen — the tides of the great Indian Ocean, unlike the still, dead waters of the Mediterranean Sea. The day after leaving Ayun-Musa was at first within sight of the blue channel of the Red Sea, but soon Red Sea and all were lost in a sand-storm, which lasted the whole day. (I have retained this account of the sand-storm, chiefly because it seems to be a phenomenon peculiar to this special region. Van Egmont, Niebuhr, Miss Martineau, all noticed it; and it was just as violent at the passage of a friend in 1841, and again of another, two months after ourselves, in 1853.) Imagine all distant objects lost entirely to view — the sheets of sand floating along the surface of the desert, like streams of water, the whole air filled with a tempest of sand, driving in your face like sleet. We were undoubtedly on the track of the Israelites; and we saw the spring which most travelers believe to be Marah, and the two valleys, one of which must almost certainly — both, perhaps—be Elim. The general scenery is either immense plains (*i. e., bare and barren plains of sand,* as described below), or, latterly, a succession of watercourses (*without water,* see below), exactly like the dry bed of a Spanish river. These gulleys gradually bring you into the heart of strange black and white mountains. *For the most part the desert was absolutely bare.* But the two rivals for Elim are fringed with trees and shrubs, *the first vegetation we have met in the desert.* First, there are the wild palms, successors of the 'threescore and ten,' not like those of Egypt or of pictures, but either dwarf—that is, trunkless—or else with savage, hairy trunks, and branches all disheveled. Then there are the feathery tamarisks, here assuming gnarled boughs and hoary heads, on whose leaves is found what the Arabs call manna. Thirdly, there is the wild acacia; but this is also tangled by its desert growth into a thicket—the tree of the burning bush and the shittim wood of the tabernacle. A stair of rock brought us into a glorious wady, inclosed between red granite mountains, descending precipitously upon the sands. I can not too often repeat that these wadys are exactly like rivers, *except in having no water;* and it is this appearance of torrent bed and banks, and clefts in the rocks for tributary streams, and at times even rushes and shrubs fringing their course, which *gives to the whole wilderness a doubly dry and thirsty aspect—signs of 'Water, water every where, and not a drop to drink.'*"

Well, I have read two or three most excellent replies to these objections, which I cordially recommend, because I do not want you to take my opinion, as if it stood alone. A most pithy reply is written by a friend of mine, Mr. Saville. A very able reply has been written by Mr. John Collyer Knight, of the British Museum. One of the most remarkable, and to me most original, and containing much suggestive matter, has been written by Dr. Beke, a member of the Geographical Society, a competent antiquarian and geographical scholar. He thinks, what is important, as coming from so good a judge, and states in his letter to the Bishop of Natal, "Now, in the first place, I can not admit that you have satisfactorily controverted Canon Stanley's argument that, during the ages which have elapsed since the Exodus, considerable changes have taken place in the physical condition of the Sinaitic peninsula. On the contrary, I believe that very great changes have taken place, and that formerly the peninsula was far less inhospitable and barren than it is at the present day. Without entering into any lengthened details, I will adduce a few instances to show that such must be the case. While writing these lines, I read in *The Times* newspaper of the 31st of October, that the British Consul at Jedda, on the Arabian coast of the Red Sea, reports that the sea on that coast is gradually receding, owing to the formation of coral reefs! This must be understood to mean, that the coral reefs formed along the coast are being brought above the surface of the sea by a gradual rising of the land, offering to the eye of an ordinary observer the appearance of the recession of the sea itself. Along the African coast of the Red Sea, the like phenomenon has been observed by myself and other travelers. And if we consider the statements of Herodotus respecting the primeval condition of Egypt, and that of Artemidorus, to the effect that a branch of the Astaboras, the Nile of the Ethiopians, sent part of its waters into the Red Sea, near Ptolemais Theron; and if further, we compare Claudius Ptolemy's description and map of the Upper Nile and its principal tributaries with the actual courses of those rivers, we must feel convinced that the same operation of nature has been going on during ages. On the eastern side of the Arabian peninsula, likewise, the Persian Gulf has for many years past been known to be rapidly becoming shallower and more limited in extent. Hitherto, the geological changes in those regions have not attracted the notice they deserve; but when the attention of geologists shall be directed to them, I have no doubt of their adopting the opinion, that within the historical period, those changes have been of sufficient amount to affect materially the physical form and condition of all those countries."

This reply to the Bishop is complete; for what is the Bishop's assumption? That in the year 1863, the peninsula of Sinai, through which the Israelites passed, is bleak, desert, inhospitable, barren, and a mass of rocks; *ergo*, says the Bishop, with a leap over 3,000 years — which is a very wide leap indeed — there was no food 3,000 years ago for the cattle of Israel. But Dr. Beke says, what Canon Stanley also hints, that there is reason to believe that the desert is not now what it was then; therefore before the Bishop can use the present deserted and bleak condition of the peninsula of Sinai as an argument against the historic truth and veracity of the Word of God, he must be prepared to prove that the peninsula of 1863 is precisely what it was 3,000 years ago. But that great changes have passed on Eastern lands may be proved by referring to the state of Palestine. What is the picture of Palestine in the Word of God? A land overflowing with milk and honey, a land so rich and so beautiful that it was the most lovely, and the most beautiful, and the most fertile of all lands. It was so upwards of 2,000 years ago. What is the condition of Palestine now? Read Lamartine or Chateaubriand on Palestine, — the most exquisite and poetical, yet historic and true descriptions that I know. What do they describe? Cloven rocks, burning sands, little stunted bits of corn, so stunted and so precarious that the sower never can calculate upon being the reaper; the hoof of the Arab steed on the hot sand; the tent of the Bedouin in the desert; the burning sun; a sky as brass; and a parched earth cloven, as it thirsts for the early and the latter rains, and does not receive them; constitute the existing condition of Palestine. Chateaubriand says, "A soft and chalky earth, which has been formed by the gradual wasting away of the calcareous rocks, swallows up our footsteps. This portion of the country is so shockingly barren, that it does not possess even the semblance of a bit of moss. One can only discover here and there some tufts of thorny plants, as pale as the soil that produced them, and covered with dust, like the trees on the sides of our highways during summer. The mountains present the same appearance, clothed in white dust, without a shade, without a tree, destitute of herbage, and not even possessing a scrap of moss."

"We perceived Jerusalem through an opening in the mountains. I did not at first know what it was. I believed it to be only a mass of shattered rocks. The sudden apparition of this city of desolations in the midst of such wasted solitudes, had something about it fearful. She was the Queen of the Desert."

Here is a parallel case. Two thousand years ago, Palestine was all that beauty, fertility, and climate could make it, or heart of inhabitant could desire. But in the present day it is a bleak, barren, wasted desert. Might not the Bishop have thought, if such a change has taken place in the case of Palestine, that it is neither singular nor solitary if the peninsula of Sinai has experienced a parallel deterioration? His reasoning is worthless, and his objections frivolous. At all events, the Bishop must prove that the peninsula of Sinai, unlike Palestine, exists to-day as during the Exodus; and to do this he must get over the facts adduced by Dr. Beke as well as those of Canon Stanley.

I will not detain the reader too long with those critical discussions, I will adduce what I think is the most conclusive evidence that the Mosaic record is historically true and inspired—the coïncidence, the marvelous coïncidence between the facts and phenomena recorded there, and their moral, spiritual, practical, and plainly intended application to the hearts and consciences of all mankind. But, before I do so, I must notice one remaining objection. The Bishop objects, at page 48, in the strongest terms, to the statement about the Exode in Exodus xiii. 18, where we read—"The children of Israel went up harnessed out of the land of Egypt." His objection is, "It is inconceivable that these down-trodden, oppressed people should have been allowed by Pharaoh to possess arms, so as to turn out at a moment's notice 600,000 armed men. If such a mighty host—nearly nine times as great as the whole of Wellington's army at Waterloo, (69,686 men, Alison's *History of Europe*, xix. p. 401)—had had arms in their hands, would they not have risen long ago for their liberty?" He forgets that the precise number of years of their captivity were settled, and settled by God; and against His decree their rebellion would have been like the waves of the sea rising in insurrection against the rooted and eternal rocks. "Or, at all events, would there have been no danger of their rising?" His objection lies against the statement that the Iraelites went forth 600,000 men, fully armed with swords, with bows, with bucklers, and all the weapons of ancient war. Our answer is complete. The word "harnessed" in the Hebrew does not mean universally or necessarily, possessed of offensive arms. The Hebrew word, as shown in numerous instances, denotes simply that they went out, in order, in array, as the Romans would say, *accincti*, not a disorderly mob, but as a regiment, corps, or battalion; whether with arms, or without arms, is not in question ; it means in perfect array, without confusion or disorder of any sort. And there are many hints scattered throughout Exodus that when war actually occurred it was a selection of picked men, and not the 600,000 who were called upon to do battle. But in this instance, too, the Bishop, from his long residence among the African Zulus, who almost made a convert of him, must have forgotten the common *usus loquendi*, or habit of speech, in modern times. If the electric telegraph were to bring news to-morrow (and it may bring the news some day) France has universally armed, of course our cabinet would instantly see that the Guards and the different regiments were all prepared to do—what they will always be ready to do—their duty. But at the same time I do not think that Lord Palmerston would ever imagine that France's arming meant that the thirty-six millions that constitute the population of that country had each shouldered an Enfield rifle, and that the whole were prepared to come down like an avalanche upon England. Nobody but the Bishop of Natal could so understand the telegraphic communication. We should suppose that a nation acting in this way meant a nation acting through its constituted and recognized right arm—its soldiers. Therefore, when it is said that the children of Israel went out from Egypt into the desert armed, taking the Hebrew word which we have translated "harnessed" in its most limited sense, all that it can mean is, that they went out with a sufficient guard, with a sufficient body of defenders, brave men, able to do battle with Pharaoh in the desert, and to defend their wives and their children, their tents and chattels, and all that they carried with them.

Having noticed these difficulties of the Bishop, I look at the great moral lessons that this must suggest to us all. First, it is said that the Israelites, as they marched out of Egypt, went out in haste. They felt they had long enough endured its burdens, toiled in its kilns, and eaten its bitter bread; and the instant that the announcement was given, or rather that the word of command was addressed to Moses, the leader of the hosts of Israel, not in confusion or dismay, but organized and disciplined, they marched in haste into the desert, and toward the land of Canaan. When the order comes from the great Captain of the Faith to come out of this world in which we are, of which we are not, will you be prepared to say "Lord, now lettest thou thy servant depart in peace, for mine eyes have seen thy salvation"?

But we read that when the Israelites went out in haste, the Egyptians, so far from interfering with their march, felt so keenly the last blow that had been struck in their homes, on their first-born throughout the whole land, that they hurried the Israelites out, saying, "We be all dead men," and they were too thankful to get rid of them as fast as possible. Our sins should drive us from ourselves; Christ's death, Christ's love, Christ's promises, Christ's care should wean and win us to Himself. Thank God, that many an Egyptian trouble beats upon us and impels us; thank God, that many a glorious promise attracts us to Immanuel's land.

It is said, in the next place, that the instant the Israelites had made up their minds to go, they "borrowed" of the Egyptians jewels, and raiment, and gold, and trinkets. The Bishop finds fault with this as incredible; but it is worthy of notice here, that the Hebrew word which our translators have translated "borrowed," literally and almost universally means *asked*, not *borrowed*. The Bishop says it is very unlikely that the Egyptian ladies would have given up their trinkets, or that they had such trinkets to give. But in the International Exhibition, you may have seen the jewels of an Egyptian lady of great rank, who lived nearly 3,000 years ago, in the right-hand gallery of the main nave; exquisite golden trinkets, of beautiful workmanship and shape, about 3,000 years old, probably similar to the very jewels which the Israelites asked from the Egyptians. There is a moral jewelry more splendid and magnificent than all the jewelry of India or of the East. An angel in the Apocalypse was struck with a spectacle such as he had never seen before — he sees a great multitude climbing up the starry steeps of heaven; arrested by their magnificence, he asks the interpreting angel, "Who are these that are arrayed in white robes, and whence came they?" Angels may at this moment be the spectators of believers performing a grander exode, climbing yet nobler steeps, and clad with white robes, and covered with jewels that glisten in the rays of an unsetting sun that by their splendor put out all the stars; and angels may ask concerning that poor woman, in that underground cellar; of that poor afflicted old man, in that garret, of whom the world says, How filthy, how poor, how wretched, how repulsive; "who are these arrayed in white robes? whence this splendor?" "These are they that came out of great tribulation;" out of garrets and underground cellars; out of dirt, and rags, and poverty, and dungeons; but "they have washed their robes, and made them white in the blood of the Lamb; and therefore they are before the throne of God, and they serve Him day and night without ceasing." "When I passed by thee none eye pitied thee, none had compassion upon thee; and when I passed by thee, and looked upon thee, it was the time of love. I spread my skirt over thee, and covered thy nakedness. I washed thee with water; I clothed thee with broidered work; I shod thee with badger's skin; I girded thee with fine linen. I decked thee also with ornaments, and I put bracelets upon thy hands, and a chain on thy neck. And I put a jewel on thy forehead, and ear-rings in thine ears, and a beautiful crown upon thine head. Thus wast thou decked with gold and silver, and thy raiment was of fine linen, and thy renown went forth among the heathen, for thy beauty; for it was perfect through my comeliness, which I had put upon thee, saith the Lord God."

Another lesson is suggested here. This great multitude marched forth from the city of Rameses to Succoth, numbering, we are told, upward of two millions of people. What a startling exodus. That passover angel, when he spread his wing, and swept through Egypt, opened all the gates of Egypt, paralyzed all the subjects of Pharaoh, and let forth out of every dungeon, and cellar, and garret, that mighty host of captives, so recently toiling in the brick-kilns, now the heirs of a glory that should not fade, and of an inheritance that should not pass away. Then was partly fulfilled what was promised to Abraham, that his seed should be countless as the stars, innumerable as the sands by the sea; and they did not retreat nor succumb until they crossed the ocean, and in the beautiful language of the fifteenth of Exodus, Miriam touched her harp, and celebrated the triumph of the Lord in the depths of the sea, and Moses sung that song which is called in the Apocalypse the song of Moses and the Lamb; and Israel learnt, "Not by might, nor by power, but by my Spirit, saith the Lord of hosts."

We are told that precisely at the end of the four hundred and thirty years, predicted as the length of their captivity, God's people Israel, that very same night, marched forth from Egypt. Here is the exact and literal fulfillment of God's Divine prediction. May we not suppose that there is here something like a warrant, not for dogmatizing, but for investigating the dates that relate to our future also? May not some of the wise and instructed Israelites, having read that God told Abraham that his children should sojourn 430 years in Egypt, have investigated the number of years they had spent in Egypt, and thence calculated how near they were to the exhaustion of the 430 years? And might they not have said to the men of the brick-kilns, and the brick-makers in the fields, "Dear Brethren, lift up your heads, your redemption draweth nigh?" This is all that students of prophecy attempt to do. If it be true that the great epochs of prophetic chronology are rapidly exhausting, and that we are every day approaching nearer to the end that will solve and explain them all; that we are already at the Saturday evening of the world's long and weary week; is it a great crime on their part to say to God's people, groaning under Egyptian bondage — in the world, not of it — weary, sorrowful, poor, oppressed, often at their wits' end, always passing through great tribulation, Dear brethren, lift up your heads, the hour of your magnificent exode is at hand, the day of your glorious deliverance dawns — a day when you will exchange the brick-kilns of Egypt for the mansions of your Father's house, and the oppression of the tyrant for the liberty wherewith Christ makes His people free?

CHAPTER VII.

THE BIBLE AND MODERN SCIENCE.

I WILL endeavor to show how scientifically ignorant the Bishop of Natal is, when he maintains that the discoveries of science are incompatible with portions of Scripture, and how scientifically correct the Scripture is wherever, in its notice of outward phenomena, it touches the confines of science. It is no doubt true the Bible was not written or intended to teach science. If we wish to be informed on geology, we must read the works of Sir Roderick Murchison, Professor Sedgwick, Hugh Miller, and other competent expositors of that science. If you wish to be informed on the subject of astronomy, you must read the productions of Herschel, Sir Isaac Newton, Madler, the Russian astronomer, and others who have distinguished themselves by their researches in the sky, and their accomplishments in that field. But if we wish to find the way to heaven, we must read the writings of Moses, of Isaiah, of Ezekiel, of St. Matthew, of St. Paul, or of "Moses and the prophets," the Gospels, and the Epistles. At the same time the Bible records, covering a period of nearly 2,000 years, must necessarily refer to many a phenomenon in nature which science has unfolded and defined. But, instead of modern science conflicting with Moses and the prophets, it will be found that wherever Moses or the writers of the Old Testament allude to phenomena in heaven or earth, or speak of the action of cause and effect in the outer world, the language employed is invariably scientifically exact. And hence my inference is, that babblings and oppositions of science, falsely so called, not true science, may be quoted as opposed to the claims of Scripture; but that true science, in its latest and most brilliant discoveries, with unhesitating voice proclaims, "Thy word, O God, is truth."

In this lecture I will bring forward illustrations of this, at least a few, as specimens of many that might be adduced, did space permit, and the occasion require it.

I will go back to the very earliest Mosaic records. It is stated unquestionably, in the opening chapter of Genesis, that light existed before the sun. A portion of the language of the opening chapter of Genesis, Longinus, an eminent rhetorician, pronounced the sublimest sentence in any language, or in any book: "And God said, Let there be light; and there was light." But, after the creation of light, we find it stated that the work of the fourth day was, "Let there be lights in the firmament of the heaven to divide the day from the night; and let them be for signs, and for seasons, and for days, and for years. And God made two great lights; the sun, the greater light, to rule the day, and the lesser light to rule the night." The usual objection is, how ignorant was Moses! He actually has the stupidity to state that there was light before the source of light was created! Can any thing be more outrageous than this! But if so outrageous, would you expect a man of common-sense to perpetrate such an outrage? If any of us had been writing about the source of light, we never should have dreamed of talking of light spreading over the earth its beautiful mantle, unless we had first stated or assumed the source of light—the sun in the sky. And therefore the very fact that Moses deliberately states there was light before the sun was appointed to give light is not the evidence of his ignorance, but a presumptive proof that there underlies it a deeper and more glorious thought. Let us ascertain how modern science justifies Moses. In an admirable volume by Kurtz, a German writer, are set forth the links of connection between the profoundest astronomical discoveries and the most simple statements of the Word of God; and what are the most recent results of modern scientific investigation. He shows that light is not necessarily dependent on the sun. Humboldt, in his "Cosmos," says—

The northern light derives most of its importance from the fact that the earth becomes self-luminous, and shows itself in itself capable of developing light; and the intensity of the terrestrial light, in cases of the brightest radiation toward the zenith, is resembled by the light of the moon in its first quarter. Occasionally printed characters are read by this polar light without difficulty.

Wagner, another German writer, speaking of the northern light, and the natives of the northern parts of Scotland, especially the Orkney and the Shetland Isles, must be able to confirm what he says:—

The northern light being an intermitting phenomenon, and exhibiting to us the change from light to darkness, independent of the sun, we may find in it an analogy to similar changes occurring upon the earth before the creation of the sun.

And lastly, Schubert, quoted by Kurtz, says:—

May not that polar light, which is called the aurora of the North, be the last glittering light of a departed age of the world, in which the whole earth was inclosed in an expanse of aërial fluid, from which, through the agency of electro-magnetic forces, streamed forth an incomparably greater degree of light, accompanied with animating warmth, almost in a similar mode to what still occurs in the luminous atmosphere of our sun?

Now, here is the very singular fact, that toward the northern regions, around the pole, we discover a perpetual light, having no dependence on, or connection with the sun. The inference of these able scientific men is, that such polar light is the last lingering memorial of a pre-Adamite world, or at least of our world before the work of the fourth day, when the sun was appointed to rule the day, and the moon to rule the night. And if so, it would justify what geologists have noticed, that many of the fossil remains of extinct species and *genera* have eyes that indicate susceptibility of light, and must have lived where there was light. Therefore we argue from the remains of the polar light shining independent of the sun, so bright that printed letters can be read in it, that there has been a light, in all probability, long before the sun's body was created, as well as long before the sun's present office was appointed; and that that light began when God said, "Let there be light, and there was light."

Having given the scientific reply, which to my mind is most conclusive, I must notice a distinction of very great importance. When it is said in the passage I have read, or rather referred to, from Genesis, "Let there be light," the Hebrew word is אוֹר.

"And God said, Let there be light אוֹר (*owr*); and there was light." But in the record of the work of the fourth day we read, "And God made two great lights," it is in the Hebrew—אֶת־שְׁנֵי הַמְּאֹרֹת וַיַּעַשׂ אֱלֹהִים (*veaasa Elohim eth-shenei hammaaroth*); where the word used is not *bara*, 'created,' but *aasa*, 'constituted,' and the word for light is not *owr*, light, as in verse 3, but *maaroth*, which means light-carriers or bearers. God, as recorded in Genesis, on the fourth day did not create the sun, for the body of the sun may have existed millions of years before, but constituted, or set the sun and the moon to be link-carriers, light-bearers, in order to illuminate the inhab itants of this globe; in other words, He did not first create the sun and the moon on the fourth day, but He so constituted them on that day that towards our economy they sustained a definite mission to reflect what He had created three days before, light upon a world that otherwise would have been in darkness.

Where it is said, He made the sun and the moon, it has been urged as an objection that He is said to make the "stars" also. Now, we can demonstrate that the fixed stars are vastly older than the globe. For instance, a star of the twelfth magnitude must have existed 4,000 years. The way we calculate is this: Light travels with tremendous velocity. I am about to state perhaps what seems a truism, and not necessary to be told to men who have read upon this subject, but I must do so for the sake of the ignorant or less instructed, to whom the objections of Dr. Colenso are directed. We know that light travels with a velocity so great, that it takes a ray of light only eight minutes to travel from the sun to this earth; so that if you look upon the sun at noonday, at twelve o'clock, you do not see the sun as he is at that moment, but as he was eight minutes before—the light taking that time to travel. Now, it can be proved that there are stars of the twelfth magnitude whose light would take about 4,000 years to travel to our earth; and there are stars that have been demonstrated by Herschel to be so distant, that a ray of light has been traveling from them for millions of years, and it has only reached our earth within the last few years. Now, if that be the case, then we know that these stars must have existed millions of years before. Then what is meant by Moses saying, "He made the sun and the moon to be light bearers, and the stars also?" The answer is, the last words are simply a supplemental remark. He made the sun and the moon to sustain a definite relation to our world and the stars; for he is speaking not of creative acts, but of relative uses. "He made the sun and the moon to be lights, and the stars also." But if it should be said that this seems to imply that He then created the stars, I answer, Job, probably as old as Moses, and whose writings on those eastern plains of Shinar are so rich and beautiful, and full of thought, expressly states that the stars existed when this earth was created; for he tells us in his 38th chapter, at the 4th verse, "Where wast thou" (God is the speaker) "when I laid the foundations of the earth; when the morning stars sang together?"—the idea being that the morning stars were present, spectators of the creation of our orb, and were not created on the fourth day, but constituted in their relation to be light reflectors to the world that now is. The heavenly bodies bear traces of being created opaque, and subsequently being made luminous, or light-giving. How does the sun give light? The most recent discoveries are, that the body of the sun is just what the language of Moses would lead us to conclude—

a dark, or opaque body, and that the way he gives light is by a luminous atmosphere. So that we infer from the language of Moses precisely what is the deduction of modern science, that God on the fourth day gathered up the scattered light, leaving about the pole a dim memorial of its existence, concentrated that light in the sun, and made the sun relatively the servant of our globe, by reflecting his light upon the world, and enabling man to read, walk, and work, and so mind the duties and fulfill the responsibilities of life.

We also read that while God on the fourth day constituted the sun and the moon to divide the day from the night, He said also, "Let them be for signs and for seasons." Ask the mariner upon the tempestuous and stormy ocean what he could do without his observations of the stars. The primeval decree of the Almighty is, that the stars shall be to the sailor on the ocean's bosom the means of determining his longitude, or his place upon the sea. So scientifically correct is Moses, so stupidly blundering are his opponents.

In the 26th page of his introduction, the Bishop states, in a foot-note, his participation impliedly in great doubts whether man be not much older than 6,000 years ago. The Bishop is the greatest living doubter upon earth. It is all doubts from beginning to end. The unhappy prelate breathes doubts, and eats doubts, and lives in doubts, till doubts seem to be assimilated to, and incorporated with his very nature. He seems to think it very doubtful whether man be only 6,000 years old. And, secondly, one of the writers of the "Essays and Reviews," Professor Jowett, a most accomplished scholar, and Professor of Greek in the University of Oxford, says, "It is possible" (now, I say it is impossible); "and it may one day be known" (I say, that at the present day it is known to be the reverse) "that mankind spread not from one, but from many centres originally;" that is, instead of one Adam and Eve, there may have been half-a-dozen scattered over the globe, each race having a distinct and independent primeval parentage. These are very grave and serious objections. My answers are not the product of my reasoning, but the conclusions of the most competent authorities. First, it has been stated by Augustine, one of the most evangelical and excellent of the Fathers, *Nullum est creaturæ genus quod non in homine posset agnosci:* "There is no kind of creature which might not be recognized in man." Umbreit, a German writer, says: "In the name of man lay the significant idea that he was the representative of the whole earth, comprehending it as its lord and ruler in his own form." Sir Charles Lyell, one of the most eminent geologists, says—and this is a conclusive answer:—"On grounds which may be termed strictly geological may be inferred the recent date of the creation of man." Professor Owen, a living eminent physiologist and comparative anatomist, says, "Man is the sole species of his genus, and the sole representative of his order." And Lawrence says, "The human species is single, and all the differences which it exhibits are to be regarded as merely varieties." And Professor Owen says again, in opposition to Darwin, that "There is furnished the confutation of the notion of the transformation of the ape into the man." Nobody nowadays, who understands the elements of geology, will deny that this earth is millions of years old—the history in Genesis being merely that of the constitution of the dynasty of man, with all that relates to it. But we maintain that the first verse in Genesis precisely describes the great geological period. "In the beginning God created the heaven and the earth."

"In the beginning." When was that? "And the Word," says John, "was in the beginning,"—*i. e.*, eternity. "In the beginning God created the heaven and the earth." When about to introduce the dynasty of man, he tells us, by Moses, that at that period "the earth was desolation and emptiness." I may call it "wreck and ruin," indicating a previous organized state, but, for some reasons we know not, then fallen into ruin. "And the Spirit of God moved upon the face of the waters;" that is, "And the Spirit of God kept fluttering like a dove on the face of the waters." Now, remember the words, "The Spirit descended upon Jesus like a dove," and you identify the Third

Person of the Trinity here indicated, as bringing all out of confusion. Then "God said, Let there be light, and there was light." Now, what we contend is, that whilst the great geological epochs demonstrate that this earth is millions — I use a rough and vague word — of years old, all geological induction demonstrates that man is not more than 6,000 years old. When I was adducing illustrations of the Flood, I brought illustrations of the occurrence of the Flood from sources that Bishop Colenso could not deny. I mentioned to you then, that, in what is called the *drift*, next to the *alluvium*, which last belongs to man, and till we come to this last portion of the earth geologists deny that there is a trace of man; and the only trace of man is found upon the mere surface of the earth; while the traces of the fish and of all the other races of creatures that once lived are found deep down in the different geological strata. So that, if we had not one word from Moses, and if Moses were altogether laid aside, we can demonstrate the untruthfulness of this statement, that man is of ancient origin, or that we sprang from different centers, or that he is above 6,000 years old as a dynasty, the date of his introduction on our orb, according to the Scripture testimony.

Having noticed these important truths, I turn to some of the minor incidental proofs of scientific accuracy of statement contained in other parts of the Scripture. Let us turn now to Leviticus. I read there, "The life of the flesh is in the blood." Where did

Moses get this information? Were it possible to ask the most accomplished surgeons of the days of Esculapius, they could give you no information. But every enlightened and intelligent surgeon of modern times will tell you that in the blood there is a living principle, and that the life of the body is derived from it. Hence the ablest medical man, when called to a patient, knows that the last thing he will do is to bleed his patient, because he takes away the capital on which he works, and on which he can draw for that patient's recovery. Nothing but the direst necessity will compel him; because modern physiological and medical science has demonstrated that Moses, in Leviticus, stated what was an actual truth, wherever he got it, and however he learnt it, that the life is in the blood.

In Deuteronomy xxxii. 2, we read, "My doctrine shall drop as the rain, my speech shall distill as the dew." These words are not vaguely used. They hold the knowledge of the most exact and accurate science. He says, first of all, "My doctrine shall drop as the rain." How does the rain fall? It drops. But what is a very recent discovery of the nature of the creation of dew? You know that when spirits are formed it is the vapor that goes off from the boiling liquid or substance that is turned into spirit, condensed by cold. Rain drops; that is literally and strictly true. How is dew created? It is literally distilled. It is the condensation of the watery vapor that floats near the surface of the earth. That was not known a hundred years ago. Then how did Moses know it? He speaks in language most exact; the rain drops, the dew is distilled. The disclosure of modern observation is that the dew does not drop, that it does not fall from the clouds, that it is the condensation of watery vapor that floats upon the surface of the earth. Therefore Moses was scientifically right, and his objectors are scientifically wrong.

Let me give you another illustration of the same thing. In Psalm cxlvii. 16, we read, "Snow like wool;" snow falling like wool. What is the meaning of this? It can not be that snow falls in the shape of wool, for every body knows that snow-flakes do not assume the shape of wool. Then what can be meant by the Psalmist saying that snow falls like wool? Snow is as essential to keep up in winter the warmth of the earth from which you expect to draw your future crops, as wool is to keep up the warmth of a sheep, and to maintain it living on the hill-side. In other words, when the frost becomes so intense that all vegetable life would be extinguished, the snow, by a beautiful process, begins to fall, covers up the earth with its flakes, and these flakes do for the earth precisely what wool does for a sheep — keeps it warm, or prevents it sinking to a temperature so far below zero that would be destructive to all vegetable life. Where did the Psalmist get this information that the snow is like wool, or why did he use an illustration that till within the last perhaps fifty or hundred years must have been thought by superficial readers absurd and unnatural? We answer that the Psalmist was scientifically right and his objectors are wrong.

I turn, in the next place, to a very remarkable passage in the Book of Ecclesiastes, full of instructive thoughts, and in the very first chapter, at the beginning. It is written there, "The words of the Preacher; vanity of vanities; all is vanity." Then the 5th verse, "The sun also ariseth, and the sun goeth down, and hasteth to his place where he arose." Let me explain that in the 6th verse the word "wind" is really a mistake. In the Hebrew it is "he," referring to what he has been speaking of previously, the sun. In the Septuagint it is expressly stated, "the sun." So let us read the two verses again: 5th verse; "The sun also ariseth, and the sun goeth down, and hasteth to his place where he arose. The sun goeth toward the south, and turneth about toward the north;" and then, "the wind whirleth about continually, and returneth again according to his circuits." Now, this language seems all perplexity and mystery till you remember the following facts. First, day and night are referred to by the appearance of the son above the horizon in his transit from the east unto the west, where he hasteneth. But in the next passage, "The sun goeth toward the south, and turneth about unto the north," we find the astronomical truth, speaking popularly, stated of the annual course of the sun. Having spoken of his daily course from the east to the west, he now speaks of his annual course. For I need not state, except for the sake of some young readers, that while the earth has a motion on its axis, rotating in twenty-four hours, it has a motion in his orbit, going over it in the course of 365¼ days. Well now, having stated his rotating on its axis in twenty-four hours, he then explains its motion in its orbit; namely, that the annual apparent course of the sun is through the twelve signs of the zodiac, advancing from the equinoctial southward to the Tropic of Capricorn, from which he turneth about to the north until he reaches the Tropic of Cancer. So that in this very passage you have, first of all, a beautiful description of the earth's rotation on its axis, or day and night; and you have, secondly, an exact scientific description of the sun marching apparently to us in his orbit, constituting in that march the varied and the beautiful seasons which we all know.

And then he adds, in the next place, "The wind whirleth about continually, and returneth again according to his circuits." What can be the meaning of this? Ask Admiral Fitzroy, a very competent authority, whose signal drum at each seaport saves many a gallant mariner from a watery grave, and many a ship from shipwreck. We have been accustomed to think that when a gale of wind blows, it starts from a point, say south-west, and it blows in a direct line north-east. Now, that is the common popular notion, and it has been for hundreds of years the common popular opinion. But what is the discovery of those who have studied it? That all storms are cycloidal, and that they come and strike in eddies and in circles, not in direct lines. In other words, they have discovered in the nineteenth century what Solomon stated 977 years before the birth of Christ, that "the wind whirleth about continually, and returneth again according to his circuits," his goings round; in other words, the cycloidal direction of storms.

Let me refer to another passage from this very chapter, again to show how scientifically correct is the language of Scripture. In the seventh verse he says, "All the rivers run into the sea, yet the sea is not full; unto the place from whence the rivers come, thither they return again." What is the meaning of this? The answer is, the aqueous circulation; only a recent scientific discovery. All the rivers, the Thames, the Mississippi, the Missouri, the Danube, the Rhone, the Rhine, the Forth, the Dee, come from the sea; and according to the language of Solomon here in this very passage, they not only all come from the sea, but they all run into the sea, and yet the sea is not full. The sun hovers over the ocean, which, with its bright, gleaming eye, ever looks up to him; he exacts from the ocean a tribute of watery vapor by the fervor of his heat; he gives the clouds charge of that watery vapor; they carry it in their fleecy folds over many a broad acre and many a lofty mountain. When the cold chill of the air in its circuits touches them, the vapor is condensed; just as if you apply a cold object to the steam rushing from a tea-kettle, it will be condensed into water. The water falls upon the hills, the hills pour down the waters in the shape of corries, as we call them in the Highlands; these corries swell into streams, these streams into great rivers, these rivers pour into the ocean; yet the ocean is not full, because it only receives what it originally gave. How literally exact is the language of the inspired writer.

Let me turn to another passage, that you may see what outrageous nonsense some men speak against the Bible. In Job xxvi. 7, we read, "He hangeth the earth upon nothing." And this is not peculiar to Job; similar expressions occur in various portions of the Old Testament Scriptures. Now, what is the opinion of the modern Hindoos? It is this; that the earth is a vast plain; that there is an ocean of milk round it, then there is an ocean of wine, then there is an ocean of butter, then an ocean of something else; but that it is one vast plain; and when they have been asked what it stands upon, they answer, upon an elephant. And what does the elephant stand upon? Upon a tortoise. But what does it stand upon? There they stop. Then what was the ancient notion of the most accomplished and gifted philosophers? Plato thought that the earth was in a state of constant oscillation; but how it was, or what its support was, they barely imagined. Then I ask you, where did Job get what to Plato, and to Socrates, and to Aristotle, would have appeared as nonsense, what the Hindoo regards as the very height of absurdity; where did Job get this information that "He hangeth the earth upon nothing?" The answer is, that the Eastern patriarch, if he did not know the great law of gravitation, at least has expressed himself by the inspiration of One that did know—precisely the disclosure of modern astronomical science—that the earth gravitates toward the sun, the central body, and that literally God has hung the earth upon nothing.

Again, Job says, "He stretcheth out tne north over the empty place." Now, we have navigators who have nearly reached the North Pole, but they knew nothing of that. What is meant, then, by Job saying, "He stretcheth out the north over the empty place?" Why "empty place" associated with the north? Sir John Herschel finds that the empty portion of the firmament, empty of stars comparatively, is at the North Pole. But how did Job know that? He that inspired him taught him to express himself in language scientifically accurate and exact.

Again, Job says, "He maketh weight for the winds." To a common mind, unacquainted with science, that would appear outrageous. Then how do you explain it? I will explain it by an incident. When Galileo was sent into prison because he had the impudence to say in the hearing of the Pope of Rome and the cardinals of that day, who, mind you, were infallible, that the sun did not go round the earth, but that the earth took the trouble of going round the sun, he was denounced by infallibility as a heretic, he was sent to prison, and subjected to the most cruel treatment, because he stated what was written long ago in the word of God, and what all science has since justified. But one day a person who was appointed to make a pump, in order to bring water out of a very deep well, came to Galileo, or rather was permitted to approach Galileo in prison, to ask him to explain how it came to pass that in this well which was only 40 feet deep, he could not get the pump to draw water so as to supply what the household required, as essential to its comfort, if not its very existence. Galileo said, "I believe it is owing, but I must not state it, or my imprisonment would continue, to the weight of the wind, or the weight of the atmosphere." And what is the fact? That the atmospheric pressure is exactly equal to a column of water of 33 feet deep; and that if you put a pump into a well 36 feet deep, it will not bring water up; but if you put a pump into a well 30, or 29 feet deep, it will bring water up. Why? Because the pressure of the atmosphere is equal to the weight of a column of water 33 feet deep. Galileo instantly guessed, or rather calculated, what must be true; and that estimate of the astronomer in prison was a brilliant commentary upon Job on the plains of Shinar, "He maketh weight for the winds." So scientifically correct is Scripture; so scientifically wrong were the infallible cardinals and pope of that day.

Let me mention another, perhaps a much smaller instance. In Job xiv. 8, we read, "Though the root thereof wax old in the earth, and the stock thereof die in the ground; yet through the scent of water it will bud, and bring forth boughs like a plant." Now, a very recent discovery, and the result of microscopic inspection, is, that the leaves of plants are respiratory organs, and in these leaves are vessels of secretion. And therefore the language of Job, that though the root has died, and though the stock thereof has failed, yet if there be leaves left, through the scent of water, the tree will bud again; that is, strictly and botanically true.

One of the prophets, Habakkuk, says, "Though the fig-tree shall not blossom." The language is peculiar, "Though the fig-tree shall not blossom." What is the fact? The edible fig is the blossom of the fig-tree; and, in strictly scientific language, the receptacle containing a large number of minute unsexual flowers growing to a succulent base. The fig-tree has no blossom; or, rather, its blossom is the fig; and therefore the language of the prophet is strictly, beautifully, and scientifically exact.

Let me quote another passage. In Job xxxviii. 31, we read, "Canst thou bind the sweet influences of Pleiades?" It long puzzled commentators to settle what could be the meaning of the influences of the Pleiades. Madler, a celebrated Russian astronomer, says, "I regard the Pleiades"—he is not speaking from a Scriptural point of view, but merely giving his independent conclusion; a conclusion formed on scientific grounds, or rather on the use of his telescope, and without the least reference to the language of Job,—

> I regard the Pleiades as the central group to the whole astral system and the fixed stars, even to its outer limits, marked by the Milky Way; and I regard Alcyone as that star of all others composing the group which is favored by most of the probabilities as being the true central sun of the universe.

Job speaks of the attractions of the Pleiades; the astronomer only the other day discovered that Alcyone, which is distant from us thirty-one and a half million times the distance of the sun from the earth, is in all probability a central sun. Who knows but there, throned in majesty, magnificence, and glory, may be He who made all, and without whom nothing was made that was made. At all events, we find, that while all the planets that constitute our solar system — the earth, the moon (its satellite), Jupiter, Saturn, Mars, and others are all revolving round the sun as their center, that our sun, with all his planets, and our earth among the rest, is but a tiny group amid thousands of vaster and more magnificent groups revolving round one central sun, Alcyone; that sun the center of the astral system. And hence the very beautiful thought, so beautifully expressed by Job, is the most exact scientific discovery — a discovery made only within the last few years.

Let me pass to another passage in Deuteronomy

xxxii. 24. I have put each down as I gathered, or found it out; I might have arranged them perhaps better, but the instruction is the same. In Deuteronomy xxxii. 24, we find this strange language, "They shall be burnt with hunger, and devoured with burning heat." Till recent discoveries in chemistry, it was matter of perplexity what could be meant by being told, "They shall be burnt with hunger." Burnt with fire we all understand; but burnt with hunger seems altogether a mystery. But it expresses the most exact scientific truth. A man that dies of hunger is literally and truly burnt to death. You ask how? Why because the atmosphere he breathes, containing oxygen — that substance that rusts iron by acting on it — if he does not take food, and therefore has no carbon furnished, which is necessary to constitute, by its contact with oxygen in the human lungs, the vital warmth of the human body, the oxygen acts upon the tissues, and upon the lungs themselves, and a man that dies of hunger is literally and truly burnt to death. That which is the most recent discovery of science was well known to Moses; and yet this rash Bishop tells us that Moses did not know science, and that to expect that he would speak scientifically exact, is to expect what is extravagant and absurd; and that he learnt in Natal a great deal more than Moses learnt from God Almighty. You yourselves can judge which speaks truth.

I will take one more passage, and then close, not from want of others, but from want of space. It is in

2 Peter iii. 10; in that memorable passage, which I have illustrated in my book, "*Redemption Draweth Nigh*," in connection with prophetic investigation. He tells us, "But the day of the Lord will come as a thief in the night; in the which the heavens shall pass away with a great noise, and the elements shall melt with fervent heat, the earth also and the works that are therein shall be burned up." Then in the 7th verse, "The heavens and the earth, which are now, by the same word, are kept in store, reserved unto fire;" literally translated, as Mr. Edward Bishop Elliot has shown conclusively in his "Horæ Apocalypticæ," "The earth that now is, being stored with fire, is reserved against the judgment and perdition of ungodly men." Now, in what respect is this correct? Will it be said by any one that the earth is stored with fire? I once said, "The earth seems a solid globe; but there is reason to believe that the whole interior of our globe is one ocean of molten or liquid fire." This was attacked as being outrageous and absurd. I put the question to Sir Roderick Murchison, "Have you any reason to believe that the interior of the earth is any thing like what I ventured to describe?" Not having the knowledge that he had, I was too happy to get the opinion of such a man. He said, "I infer from the increase of temperature in deep shafts, and also from former and present outbursts of igneous matter, that the existence of a central heat can not, in my opinion, be denied."

Sir David Brewster, one of the most accomplished

philosophers of the day, stated to the University of Edinburgh only last year,—"Imprisoning under its elastic crust fire and water, and other elements of danger, their explosive forces are exhausted in the earthquake, and find vent in the volcano—the safety-valve of the great caldron which boils beneath our feet."

And a very eminent geologist says that, to him, "It is a marvel that there is not a conflagration every day;" and the induction of all that have studied the subject is just what I ventured to state. Awful thought! The very earth on which our houses, and our castles, and our banks, and our warehouses are built, is just a charged live shell. The mere surface, a few thousand feet in depth, is the shell; but the interior, some 7,000 miles diameter, is one ocean of surging fire: and God has only to withdraw the repressive force, and the elements shall melt with fervent heat, and the earth and the things that are therein shall all be burned up.

Let me also notice, in the next place, the expression, that "the heavens," meaning the atmosphere, "shall pass away with a great noise." The moment that such a catastrophe shall take place, the result, from the union of oxygen with hydrogen, and other gases liberated by intense heat, will awaken the most tremendous and overwhelming crashes, and sounds, and thunder, that ever reverberated in the universe. And when Peter says that "the elements shall *melt* with fervent heat," see how scientifically exact is the language of the Apostle. "Shall melt." The iron on your streets is melting. What is rust?—Burning. Every element has been burnt. Rust is simply the result of the oxygen of the air burning up the iron. If the Apostle had said, "The elements shall burn," every scientific man would have said, How ignorant Peter must have been! Why, the granite has been melted already, it was once liquid. The iron, the gold that you find in the quartz, in the crevices and fissures of the rock, it has been melted already. And therefore, in language exactly scientific, Peter says, not they shall be burnt, but "they shall melt with fervent heat."

Now, I will not dwell longer upon these, except to say that geology comes up from its secret recesses laden with its richest and its most recent phenomena, and says, "Thy word, O God, is truth." Astronomy comes down from sweeping through infinite space, weighing and counting the stars in their courses, and says, "Thy word, O God, is truth." And the hearts and the consciences of Christendom, the thousands that the Bible has enlightened, the hearts it has cheered, the consciences it has pacified, the souls it has filled with hopes that can not die, say from their deepest experience, "Thy word, O God, is truth." It will be demonstrated, the longer that the world lives, how exactly the inspired penmen wrote—how rashly a bishop and his followers have spoken.

It is important to repeat that the Bible was neither meant nor inspired to teach geology, astronomy, or botany. These sciences rest on human observation and induction. But it is alike interesting and useful to notice that Scripture in none of its allusive references to natural phenomena does violence to what the telescope of the astronomer or the hammer of the geologist has disclosed, and that many of the expressions employed by the sacred penmen fully cover — if, indeed, they do not designedly contain — the ripest and most recent conclusions of scientific research. In this respect alone it stands high as heaven is above the earth — above and apart from the Shasters of India, the astrologies of Egypt, the astronomy of Ptolemy, or the cosmology of the Greeks. Science has nothing to fear from the Bible, and the Bible has nothing to fear from science.*

* See for scientific and monumental illustrations of Scripture an able work, entitled, "Science and Revealed Religion," by the Rev. B. Saville.

CHAPTER VIII.

MOSES A PREACHER OF CHRIST.

The author of the work on which in successive lectures I have made some strictures, regards Moses very much as a myth, or of doubtful existence, and if he did exist, that he did not write the Pentateuch; and if he wrote any portion of the Pentateuch, it was a compilation of fables, traditions, stories, drifted along the currents of the world, which he worked up and pieced together after his own fancy, and according to his own taste. The Saviour, however, states (John v. 46, 47) that so intimately connected is belief in the divine legation of Moses, the ancient servant, with faith in Himself, the Lord, that the repudiation of such belief is logically followed by a rejected Lord, and a repudiated Gospel. Belief in what Moses wrote is distinctly and necessarily connected with faith in what Jesus is. If, then, Moses wrote fables, if he was a compiler of idle and unhistoric tales, borne down on the traditions of this present world, how can we justify the Redeemer's words, how can we believe that "The Truth" accepted testimony from a mere romancist; that the Prince of glory recognized a tale-writer as a witness to his greatness and his mission? The Bishop, like the Jew in the days of our Lord, rejects Moses; and if his logic halts not in its march, it must necessarily lead him to reject Christ and Christianity. According to the Saviour's words, Genesis and Revelation, the Old and the New Testaments, are intimately and inseparably linked together. Moses, the servant, and Christ, the master, bear definite and indestructible relations the one to the other. In his words the Redeemer recognizes Moses as a personal existence; he recognizes certain writings also, for he uses the word "wrote" or "writings" as associated with the name and the pen of Moses; and so recognizing them he recognizes the Pentateuch as part of the inspired word of God. The Saviour asserts, "He wrote of me." If Moses was a collector of ancient and broken traditions, which had no foundation in fact, or in authentic history; if his writings are no more historical than the "Pilgrim's Progress," or any similar book got up for instruction, but not based on historic fact, how can we explain the Redeemer's words? What sermon could the Bishop of Natal preach upon these two texts, "He wrote of me." "If ye believe not his writings, how shall ye believe my words?" So clearly has Moses written, so intelligible does his writing still remain, that the man who is most intimately versed in the writings of Moses will be the readiest to receive the office, and the teaching, and the character of Jesus.

In what sense or shape did Moses write of Him? First, he must have received special inspiration from on high to be able to do so; and, secondly, from distinct and expressive references contained in the New Testament scriptures and quotations from his writings and allusions to the symbols and types he employs, we learn that there is a gospel according to the Pentateuch, as true and as real as the gospel according to St. John, but not so clear, because life and immortality were not then so fully brought to light.

Moses lived some 1,400 years before the birth of Christ. His writings had been in the hands, I might say, in the hearts, unquestionably in the homes of the Jews for upwards of a thousand years. And so clearly and cogently, according to the Saviour's own statement, did he write of Jesus, that if you will not receive the photograph you must reject the original. He who repudiates the inspired artist's creation, done 1,400 years before, can not recognize the grand original, when he breaks upon the world like the sun in his morning brightness. Where then does Moses speak, or rather write of Christ? If he does so at all, he must have had celestial guidance to portray what was not yet actual; his pen must have conducted down an inspiration that directed him to record and sketch the likeness of the Son of God. Moses could not have seen Christ, for he was not yet born in the flesh. He could not have guessed, for the touches are too exact, the likeness too perfect; it is impossible to believe that Moses could have stumbled accidentally upon a picture which the more it is examined and compared with the grand original, turns out to be visibly more and more the impress of a divine and inspired guidance. The fact that Moses so wrote of Christ is proof that Moses must have been inspired. But what makes the discovery of the imposture possible and easy, if imposture there was, is the fact that "he *wrote*," that the language of the Redeemer is "his writings." Now, had it been a floating tradition, handed from mouth to mouth along the successive generations of the Jewish people, it might have become brighter as the rising sun came nearer, and it might have been retouched by the ingenuity of those that wished to show that the one was a prediction of the other. But we know that his writings existed in all their integrity, almost contemporaneously with the Hebrew commonwealth. We know that nearly 300 years before the birth of our Saviour, the Old Testament was translated into Greek, and in the Septuagint form it exists at this moment, accessible to every one who can read that language. Moses therefore was committed to the issues of his having written what he believed to be the picture of Christ, and he left us the means of ascertaining how far he prophesied what was actual historic truth, or how far he drew upon his imagination for fanciful forms with which to charm a people, and create a wild and delusive hope which could not be realized. Take, therefore, the portrait of Jesus, as sketched by the pen; or, if you like, drawn by the pencil of Moses; and take the portrait of Jesus, as given in the gospel of Matthew, where we have one profile; in Luke the opposite profile; in Mark a three-quarter face; in John the perfect fullness and the inner depths of that heart of hearts, and the infinite wisdom of One who spake as never man spake, and loved as never man loved. Take the full and perfect picture of Jesus sketched by the four Evangelists; compare what Moses wrote with what they have written; and if Moses did not sketch what is justified by what they have written, then Moses was a false prophet; and Bishop Colenso is right, and Moses is altogether wrong.

I proceed to adduce the instances of allusion to Christ by Moses. I will here notice a very interesting fact; I will not say an intentional prediction of the Saviour, but certainly a coïncidence so vivid and remarkable, that I think it is not unlikely a prophecy. If we turn to the 5th chapter of the Book of Genesis, we shall find there the names of the antediluvian patriarchs, beginning with Adam and ending with Noah: in the 3d verse, Adam and Seth; in the 6th verse, Enos: in the 9th, Cainan; in the 12th, Mahalaleel; in the 15th, Jared, or Yared; in the 21st, Enoch; in the 25th, Methuselah; in the 26th, Lamech; and in the last verse of all, Noah. It is most remarkable, that if we translate these ten Hebrew names, from Adam to Noah, we shall find that literally translated from the Hebrew, they are as follows:—Adam, "man in the image of God;" Sheth, "substituted by;" Enos, "man in misery;" Cainan, "lamenting;" Mahalaleel, "the blessed God;" Yared, "shall come down;" Ænoch, "teaching;" Methuselah, "his death will send;" Lamech, "to the humble;" Noah, "rest, or consolation." These names, designedly or undesignedly I can not venture to say, are laden with the most precious and distinctive truths of Christianity, and form a prophecy from the pen of Moses, of the nature of that sacrifice in which he trusted, and in which we glory.

The next writing of Jesus to be found in the pages of Moses, is in the promise, "He," the seed of the woman: not "she," as the Roman Catholics unhappily translate it in their translation from the Vulgate. The Hebrew pronoun is masculine, not feminine. In the Septuagint translation it is in the masculine gender also. And therefore the English authorized version gives the just translation; "He," the seed of the woman, "shall bruise thy head," speaking to the serpent, "and thou shalt bruise his heel." Explain the words, and they mean this: that some one descended of the woman should crush the head of, that is, vitally wound, the treacherous serpent, Satan; and that this one who should thus crush the serpent's head, should in the achievement of the victory suffer partial and temporary crippling, if I may use the word, in his heel; so that the ultimate march to victory and universality of the gospel of Christ should so far be impeded. That this was not a mere random prediction is plain from allusions to it in subsequent portions of the Book of Genesis. "In thy seed," the same, the woman's seed, "shall all the nations of the earth be blessed." Again, in Genesis xii. 3,—"In thee," speaking of a person, "shall all families of the earth be blessed." Here, then, is the very first preaching of the gospel under the shadow of the walls of Paradise, and amidst the chill that fell upon two human hearts when sin disturbed the conscience, darkened the mind, and brought clouds in the sky, and mists upon the earth, and gave startling and impressive testimony that a great catastrophe had overtaken the dynasty of man. Was this promise fulfilled? It was that on which humanity kept afloat for 2,000 years before the deluge; it was that to which the eyes and the hearts of Israel looked, and the world's gray fathers clung, amidst dreary and dark and desolate ages; and it is that which the writers in the New Testament expressly justify as a prediction of the advent of Christ. For, in Galatians iv. 4, it is written, "When the fullness of the time was come, God sent forth His Son, made of a woman." But that text is inexplicable, unless in the light of what Moses wrote concerning Christ. Again, we are told in 1 John iii. 8: "The Son of God was manifested, that he might destroy the works of the devil." If we

8*

take these two texts, we shall find they are just the historic statement of the fulfillment of what Moses wrote, or rather what Moses records of what God said 4,000 years and upwards before the Christian era. And what is a sort of collateral, though not in itself a reliable proof of the reality of this allusion, is the fact that Volney, the infidel writer, who had no taste and no love for authentic Christianity, reports, "There exists a tradition every where in antiquity of the expected conqueror of the serpent, a Divine person, born of a woman, who was expected to come." The "Edinburgh Review" says, "The miraculous conception of the Great Deliverer was widely known in the world before the birth of Christ." The Grecian Hercules, half human, half divine, subduing the hydra by his strength, and dying by its poison, was a distorted caricature of the great Conqueror, or the great Bruiser of the serpent's head. The Indian or Hindoo incarnation of Deity, the virgin-born Krishna, slaying the serpent, and wounded by it in the heel, is another broken tradition of the same great truth. These distorted traditions, like the Polar light in Northern realms, indicate the setting of a light that once shone, and are in their measure predictions and earnests of a light that will yet rise, and shine from sea to sea, and from the river to the ends of the earth. Study, then, that promise given by Moses of the woman's seed; study the promise of what he is to do; turn to the references found in the pages of the inspired writers of the New

Testament, and we become sure that Moses wrote of Christ. If Moses then and there has recorded a mere fable, how will the Bishop justify St. Paul in stamping it with the impress of his authority; how will he justify John in his epistle in referring to it as fulfilled in the Saviour's work? How will he vindicate the Saviour himself?

I take a step farther. There is found in Genesis the indication of the time when the Saviour should be made manifest; and that the Saviour, a man, and yet greater than man, for He was to do what man was unable to do in innocence, should bruise the serpent's head. There is also given us a clue to the identification of the promised man; for he tells us the time of his advent will be when the sceptre shall have departed from Judah, and a law-giver from between his feet. He says the Messiah shall not come till the scepter shall have departed from Judah; that is, till Judah shall have lost its autonomy, or its independent self-government, and shall become a province of an empire, and tributary to a superior lord; and when Judah shall have no power of making laws irrespective of its foreign ruler, and no one within its own bounds shall retain legislative functions, but merely the executive of laws made by the supreme Cæsar; Judah being reduced to the dimensions of a province. Does history justify the prophecy? We find that at the time the Saviour came, the decree of Augustus was accepted and recognized as a superior order to enroll the people;

that the current coin of the realm bore the image and the superscription of Cæsar, and that the Jews themselves admitted they had lost their autonomy, or power of independent self-government; for they could not put any man to death, nor execute a criminal for the greatest crimes of which he might be guilty. I do not say that Moses gives his birthplace; but the prophets do; Micah proclaimed that Bethlehem should be his birthplace. I notice one other trait given by Moses; for I must restrict myself to the predictions contained in the writings of Moses, according to the Saviour's statement, "he wrote of me." I quote from Deuteronomy xviii. 15, these words: "The Lord thy God will raise up unto thee a Prophet from the midst of thee, of thy brethren, like unto me; unto Him ye shall hearken." Now does this or does it not refer to the Son of God, the Saviour of sinners? If it does not, then Stephen, the proto-martyr, died believing in a myth, and the Bishop is so far justified in saying that Moses did not testify of Christ; for St. Stephen says, in Acts vii. 37, "This is that Moses, which said unto the children of Israel, A prophet shall the Lord your God raise up unto you of your brethren, like unto me; him shall ye hear." Peter repeats the same in Acts iii. 20, 22, where he dilates upon it; for he says, "And he shall send Jesus Christ, which before was preached unto you; whom the heaven must receive until the times of restitution of all things, which God hath spoken by the mouth of all His holy prophets since the world began. For," laying the stress of the personality and of the advent of Christ upon a testimony in Deuteronomy, "Moses truly said unto the fathers, A prophet shall the Lord your God raise up unto you of your brethren, like unto me; him shall ye hear in all things whatsoever he shall say unto you. And it shall come to pass, that every soul, which will not hear that prophet, shall be destroyed from among the people."

Let us also mark the confirmatory proofs of the same great fact in the constant allusions throughout the Gospels by those who themselves did not universally believe in him as the Messiah. For instance, in Luke vii. 16, we read, "A great prophet is risen up among us." Again, in John vi. 14, "This is of a truth that prophet that should come into the world." Why the definite article, "*that* prophet?" He means that prophet predicted by Moses. When John was interrogated, the people said to him, "Art thou that prophet?" They had many prophets; why this specific and definite reference to some one prophet in particular? It was the Jew remembering the promise on which his fathers had rested for many hundred years, and anxious to know if that promise had been translated into fact, and had become personated in Jesus Christ of Nazareth. Again, the question is, "Art thou that prophet which should come into the world?" Again, John vii. 40; "Of a truth this is the prophet." Again, Matthew xxi. 11: "This is Jesus the prophet." Now all these passages most emphatically prove that those that did not receive Jesus as the Messiah, believed that these words were a prediction of a Messiah that was to be, and that those who were inspired of God, and competent to speak what was its reference, its significance, and its application, have said with one concurrent testimony that Moses thus spoke or wrote of Christ.

I might show still farther the force of this by drawing, did space permit, a parallel between Moses and Christ. They were like in dignity,—" A prophet like unto me." The apostle says, " Moses verily was faithful in all his house as a servant; but Christ as a son over his own house; whose house are we." Moses was a legislator, and the mediator of *a* covenant; Jesus is *the* Legislator, and the Mediator of a better covenant. The law of Moses was coëxtensive with the chosen nation; the law of Jesus covers the area, and is coëxtensive with the whole population of the globe. Moses instituted the Passover; led the people through the desert; fed them miraculously with manna; was their advocate and their intercessor. All these points might be worked out in detail, and the evidence brought irresistibly forth that Moses wrote of Christ, was therefore inspired when he did so, because only one guided by a supernatural light could portray One who was to appear 1,400 years afterwards, " the light that lightens the Gentiles and the glory of his people Israel." In the words of Dr. Jortin, one of the most eminent divines of a former day in the Church of England, "Is this similitude and correspondence between Moses and Christ in so many particulars the effect of mere chance? Let us search all the records of universal history, and see if we can find a man so like to Moses as Christ. If we can't find such a one, then we have found Him of whom Moses in the law and the prophets did write, to be Jesus of Nazareth, the Son of God." Here then you have another proof that Moses wrote of Christ. And again, I repeat, because in the day in which we live it is important to repeat it, that Moses must have been inspired; that therefore what Moses wrote is not fable, is not tradition, is not unhistorical; but sober, and authentic, and reliable history.

The present day, I need scarcely add, is the era of reäction. It is the ebb-tide of a state that existed some fifteen or twenty years ago. Then the tide was flowing full and strong toward Rome, and the Pope, and Popish rites, and Popish ceremonies, and Popish doctrines, were quite the rage and the fashion. Such of us as denounced the tendency as incipient apostasy from the truth were of course set down as fanatics, ultra-Protestants, and fools. The tide now has ebbed away, and sets in fast into the Dead Sea. There is spreading in England, and in Scotland, and in more denominations than one, a sympathy with what is called Broad Churchism; that means a church so broad that it comprehends Christ, and Belial, and the Pope, and would comprehend Mahomet, I dare say, if it were sufficiently genteel. There is a disastrous tendency among many to grind down the distinctive truths of Protestant and evangelical Christianity. Now, just as I contended with all my might, however feebly, against those that would corrupt these glorious truths by the addition of that which is human, or by Popish traditions, so I would contend against those who would undermine and sap these glorious truths by denying the inspiration of their record, and explaining them away. It is matter of thankfulness to God that in the Church of Scotland, and in the Church of England there are Articles, and Confessions, and Standards that remain, clear and decisive, and of no uncertain sound; it is a grand fact, however some may dislike it, that those precious Articles and Confessions are part and parcel of the constitution of the land, and not subject to the oscillations of restless opinion. Therefore, how any one holding the sentiments of Bishop Colenso can possibly, for instance, sign the Thirty-nine Articles (than which I do not know a more precious testimony to vital truth, in opposition to deadly error), or the standards of any Church of the Reformation; how that Bishop, for instance, can go into the Church of England, and say, "O God the Father, have mercy upon us; O God the Son, have mercy upon us;" for he must be an idolater if he means what he prays and yet believes Jesus not to be God; for he can not believe that that Saviour was God who was not better informed than cotemporary adults of his nation, and needed to grow in instruction just as they did and we do. But these old grand truths, these great and essential Protestant truths, are the truths to live by, and the only truths to die in. And depend upon it, what the Scottish, and English, and Continental Reformers excavated from the rubbish of Rome, and what those great men, the Puritans of England, preached—whether in the Church or out of it is of no consequence—this old-fashioned, evangelical, Protestant Christianity is substance and life; and depend upon it nothing will stand a death-bed, and a judgment-seat, or appease a troubled conscience, or comfort a desolate heart, short of these precious truths. The Holy Ghost has inspired, and the experience of ten thousand hearts has justified them as the wisdom of God and the power of God unto salvation.

But I take a step farther in the direction in which I have been reasoning, and notice the remarkable words contained in Scripture, in Hebrews iv. 2: "Unto us was the gospel preached, as well as unto them." The apostle Paul says the gospel was preached to the Jews. In Galatians iii. 8, he says, "The Scripture, foreseeing that God would justify the heathen through faith, preached before the gospel unto Abraham." In a book that I wrote, I spoke of "that eminent Christian, Abraham." Somebody sent me a weekly newspaper that made a half page of merriment at my expense, for talking of Christianity existing in the days of Abraham. My argument and my conviction, still undiminished, was, and is, that Christianity was cotemporaneous with the wreck of Paradise; that no sooner did man fall than God Himself became the evangelist, God Himself the text, God Himself the salvation of His ruined people. The gospel then was preached to Abraham, it was preached also to the Jews. And what was that gospel preached to them? What is meant by the word *gospel?* Good news, glad tidings. Then Moses wrote and Moses preached the gospel to his cotemporaries, and in his writings to his own people that succeeded him. And what did he preach? Everlasting life, the issue of the acceptance of Christ crucified. "At thy right hand there is fullness of joy, and pleasures for evermore." I know that it is argued against the teaching of Moses, and as a disproof of his ever having taught the gospel, that he did not proclaim distinctly a future state. I maintain he did. But so far as it was a theocracy, so far as he was the prime minister of Him who was the Divine Ruler, Moses enacted temporal laws for the punishment of temporal crimes. But in the magnificent predictions, in many of the hymns and divine songs, and certainly in the Psalms, one of which at least Moses wrote, we read of fullness of joy and pleasures for evermore at God's right hand. And the very words that Moses employs, describing the deaths of the patriarchs, imply and involve the reality of eternal life. Then they preached also in that day the way to eternal life through the shedding of blood; they preached the necessity of fitness for it by taking away the heart of stone, and giving for it a heart of flesh; and they showed by the most exquisite and expressive sculpture, by the most beautiful word-paintings, how a man was to be saved.

Take the first—the cities of refuge. (Joshua xx. 2–7.) A man killed another unawares. These cities of refuge were so distributed upon mountain heights throughout the length and breadth of Palestine, from the Mediterranean to the Jordan, and from Lebanon down to the Dead Sea, that wherever the homicide was, he could see, glistening in the rays of rising and setting suns, a city of refuge to which he might flee. If the avenger of blood, that is, the nearest relative of the party slain, overtook the homicide before he got within the city of refuge, he might kill him; but if the homicide reached the city of refuge, the man that pursued him, ready to strike him dead outside, religiously abstained from touching him the instant he had crossed the threshold.

So we may have strong consolation, who have fled for refuge, to lay hold upon the hope, that is, Christ, set before us. We well remember how Moses preached Christ by the serpent of brass. (Numbers xxi. 6–9.) The Israelites were stung by a poisonous fiery flying serpent; the wound was death, and no human antidote or skill could heal it. What did Moses do? He was commanded to raise a brass serpent on a pole; and God said, now, every one that will look upon that brass serpent shall instantly get bodily health. And it came to pass that whoever looked rose to his feet, and was instantly well. Now, if I applied this arbitrarily, you might say, that is forcing Moses to write of Christ. But the great Master, who can not err, has said, "As Moses lifted up the serpent in the wilderness, that whosoever looked was healed, so also must the Son of man be lifted up, that whosoever" looketh by faith, "believeth on him may not perish, but have everlasting life." (John iii. 14, 15.)

Moses beautifully preached the gospel, as I showed you in a previous Lecture, in the Passover Lamb, the most exquisite figure and symbol, full of personal, practical, and precious significance. The family within felt their whole safety dependent, not upon the thickness of the walls, not upon the bolts of the doors, not upon the weapons they could wield, but upon this, the most unlikely thing upon earth, the blood of a lamb shed into a basin, and sprinkled on the lintels and door-posts. And the persons that were within, when they heard the beat of the angel's wing, and the wild wail that rose from contiguous homes as the first-born of Egypt were struck dead, felt that their safety was not in the strength of their walls, nor in the secrecy of their retreat, nor in the thickness of the bolts and bars, but only in the blood that was sprinkled on the door-posts. So that gospel which was preached by Moses I preach also: your safety from the destroying curse you are under, your absolute and indefeasible safety at the great white throne, is not in what you have done, is not in what you have paid, is not in what you are, but only in the blood upon the lintels of the heart, and when God shall see the blood there He will pass by. "Christ our Passover is sacrificed for us."

I might also refer to the high priest, and to other types of a similar kind.

In the words therefore of Dr. Vaughan, late head master of Harrow, who has written upon this subject:—"On what grounds are we asked thus (practically) to discard an integral portion of the Bible? There may be novelty in the voice which speaks to us," that is, the Bishop of Natal; "but there is little novelty in the objections adduced, or the main arguments by which they are supported. Some of them are as old as Christianity itself; questions asked in every nursery; registered (some of them) as difficulties in every thoughtful mind. And some things have now been worked out and exhibited in detail, which before lay, so far as English students were concerned, undeveloped and in the grave. Of this kind are those numerical difficulties in the history of the Exodus, or the arrangements of the sacrificial worship, which have now been drawn out before us almost with an air of triumph, contrasting somewhat strangely with the anxieties of the stake at issue, and the expressions of personal sorrow with which the discussion is introduced. A series of apparent discrepancies in the arithmetical computations of the Pentateuch, resting for the most part on the basis of a single fundamental number, and capable to that extent at least of reconciliation, on the supposition of a single clerical error in a department peculiarly liable to mistake, discrepancies, of which none are decisive, no, not if they were multiplied tenfold, except on the theory of inspiration, which I will venture to say is no part of the doctrine of the Catholic Church, put together by a skilled hand, and reïterated with a wearisome and almost puerile pertinacity, form the chief argument from that conclusion which is placed in the forefront of the inquiry, that the Books of Moses and of Joshua are unhistorical in their character; if the term fictitious is withheld, it is only to avoid the appearance of charging them with a fraudulent design."

But we have seen sufficient proof that there is a Gospel according to Genesis; we have no less clearly seen thus far that Moses wrote of Christ; we have also proved that Moses preached the Gospel; we have, therefore, justly concluded that the objector of Natal, however subtle, is altogether wrong; and Moses, God's ancient servant, comes out from the ordeal, the severest that can possibly be, a minister of Christ, a teacher of truth, an inspired writer in the Old Testament Scripture. The whole Bible is of God, or none of it is divine. It is so fixed together that like an arch, drop one stone, not merely the keystone, and all must come down. Blessed be God, that the evidence of its inspiration is so accessible and so great. Blessed be God, that many of us can say, it is not a matter of doubtful belief, but of absolute assurance, that Christ is the only Saviour — only and all-sufficient. Blessed be God, that even this minister of religion, consecrated and ordained to teach a very different theology, with all his subtilty, and tact, and reasoning, and learning, can not and will not, nor ten thousand abler and more learned than he, shake our belief in this book as having God for its author from Genesis to Revelation, truth for its matter, and revealing a happy meeting with all we love, and that have left and gone before us, when this weary world shall be ended, and a brighter and a better shall rise out of it.

Thus the writings of Moses form an integral part of the sacred canon, and of those records of which the inspired apostle has said, "From a child thou hast known the holy Scriptures, which are able to make thee wise unto salvation through faith which is in Christ Jesus. All Scripture is given by inspiration of God, and is profitable for doctrine, for reproof, for correction, for instruction in righteousness: that the man of God may be perfect, thoroughly furnished unto all good works."

The ancient Jew, who learned the way of life, learned it from "Moses and the prophets." Moses was a Christian man, and a Christian minister, and that too of no common type. His creed, and convictions, and character, and whole life, are inextinguishable evidences of this. His decision, in circumstances of severe trial, is a lasting proof that his religion was not in word only, but in power. He has an illustrious place among the worthies enrolled by St. Paul: "By faith Moses, when he was come to years, refused to be called the son of Pharaoh's daughter; choosing rather to suffer affliction with the people of God, than to enjoy the pleasures of sin for a season; esteeming the reproach of Christ greater riches than the treasures of Egypt: for he had respect unto the recompense of the reward." (Hebrews xi. 24—26.)

Moses not only wrote of Christ, but to Him "to live was Christ, and to die was great gain." How he could have thus believed, and lived, and died, and yet have palmed fables on mankind for facts, it must puzzle even the Bishop of Natal to explain.

CHAPTER IX.

THE PENTATEUCH PART OF THE RULE OF FAITH.

We have a most instructive historic statement of what the inmates of heaven think of Moses. It is not what the Bishop thinks. "Then he said, I pray thee therefore, father, that thou wouldest send him to my father's house: for I have five brethren; that he may testify unto them, lest they also come into this place of torment. Abraham saith unto him, They have Moses and the prophets; let them hear them. And he said, Nay, father Abraham: but if one went unto them from the dead, they will repent. And he said unto him, If they hear not Moses and the prophets, neither will they be persuaded, though one rose from the dead."—Luke xvi. 27—31.

It has been alleged by the misguided prelate, to whom I have made so frequent, though I hope not offensively personal reference, that it is doubtful if Moses existed at all; that in all probability he was a myth of the past; that if he did exist, he was not the author of the Pentateuch — and to use the defence which we often find pleaded in courts of justice, if he was the author of the Pentateuch, that he collected such fables and traditions — the waifs and strays as it were of history — as he found floating on the currents of the world, and that he wove them together, or pieced them, and made them into what is now assumed to be a continuous and inspired history by those foolish and unenlightened people called evangelical Christians and modern Protestants. This is substantially the belief of this prelate. How, I ask, is it possible to reconcile it with the words of the parable I have read? Who is the speaker? Not a fallible man, speaking amidst the shadows, and the clouds, and the prejudices of this world; but the ancient patriarch speaking from the heights of heaven, where they no longer see through a glass darkly, where there are no prejudices to dim the eye, no passions to warp the heart; where they see as they are seen, and know even as they are known. That patriarch, from the heights of heaven, in the hearing of the universe—for the Bible is as a whispering gallery in which the echoes of his voice are perpetuated—pronounces Moses an historic person, and the words of Moses to constitute a part of the rule of faith, and law of a believer's life.

If the Bishop of Natal will not hear Ezekiel, and has no ear to be charmed by the strains of David's harp, nor will regard the dying testimony of St. Stephen, nor listen to the powerful and inspired logician, the Apostle Paul, let him listen to a voice sounding down the starry steeps of heaven, perpetuated along the centuries as amid the corridors of a great cathedral, telling him that Moses wrote, and that the writings of Moses were sufficient to make men wise unto salvation.

But if this were Abraham's testimony alone, I would not ask the Bishop so earnestly to accept it; it is more, far more; for this story, recorded in this chapter, bears the signature of the Son of God. It is not a tale selected from obsolete traditions; it is not a story got up by an Æsop, or a Phædrus, or some compiler and collector of fables; it is historic truth, narrated by "The Truth;" it is a painting portrayed by Him who made the heavens and the earth, and lighted up both with all their distinctive splendors. Abraham's testimony, to use the language of modern law, is countersigned by the signature, and invested with the authority of Jesus Christ. "They have Moses and the prophets; let them hear them. If they hear not them, neither will they be persuaded though (if) one rose from the dead."

Let us try to measure the force of this. I do not urge these things merely as a reply to Bishop Colenso; I seize the opportunity of the popularity, the striking popularity, of his most sophistical and unworthy objections to the Pentateuch,—that is, to the Word of God,—in order to enable me to show on what strong foundations that Word rests; and to enable those, whom I am bound to teach the way of all truth, to be ready every one to give an answer to the skeptic for the faith as well as the hope that is in him. Let us now see what these words imply and teach. First of all, the language of Abraham implies that Moses was the writer of the books that bore of old, and bear still his name. He says, "They," these five brethren that are on earth, "have," what every Jew recognized as inspired, "Moses and the prophets." The rich man answered, "Nay, father Abraham; but if one went unto them from the dead they will repent. And he said unto him, If they hear not;" what an attestation to the fullness, and the clearness, and the sufficiency of Moses; —"If they hear not Moses and the prophets, neither will they be persuaded, though (or if) one rose from the dead." In what shape could these five brethren left on earth have had Moses and the prophets? Personally, Moses and the prophets were in heaven; how then could they have them? In this sense: they had the writings which unfolded the mind, expressed the sentiments, and contained the history and doctrines which Moses was raised up to teach. If, for instance, you were to hear me say to a person, you have Homer, and Virgil, and Milton, what would you understand? Certainly this: You have the "Iliad" of Homer, the "Æneid" of Virgil, and the "Paradise Lost" of Milton. In the same manner when Abraham said to the rich man, "They have Moses and the prophets," he meant, they have Genesis, Exodus, Leviticus, Numbers, Deuteronomy; the five books called the Pentateuch, which Moses wrote, and in which, being dead, he yet speaketh to the heart, the conscience, and the intellect of mankind.

It is important to notice, in the second place, the very important inference which this recognition of the writings of Moses demands. It implies that these writings were able then, and I maintain they are able now, not so clearly as the gospels, but with equal certainty, to make wise unto salvation. "All scripture is given by inspiration of God, and is profitable for doctrine, for correction, and for instruction in righteousness, that the name of God may be perfect, thoroughly furnished unto all good works." It is, "all scripture is" (θεόπνευστος) "breathed into by God." These words were written by an apostle; his reference was not to the Gospels, only one of which probably was then written; nor to the Epistles, but to the Old Testament Scriptures. That it was to the Old Testament Scriptures is plain, from what he tells Timothy in the preceding verse: "From a child thou hast known the Holy Scriptures, which are able to make thee wise unto salvation." But what Scriptures did Timothy know as a child? Those which his mother and his grandmother, Lois and Eunice, taught him; those of Moses and the prophets; and on these the apostle passes the indefeasible and conclusive judgment, they are inspired or breathed into by the Spirit of God.

This rich man, lost and ruined, in misery, without hope, and without heart, and without the prospect or the possibility of deliverance, feels deep sorrow for five of his brethren, the children of the same parents, left upon the earth, and living, as he had lived, in the enjoyment of the luxuries of the world, and in utter contempt or disregard of the truths of God, of the soul, of eternity. He says, I am lost because I knew not the way to heaven, or rather neglected the great salvation. But I have an earnest desire that those I have left behind me may never come into such a place of torture as I find this to be. A sentiment or statement that does not seem compatible with what the Bishop holds, that hell is a mere purgatory; or with what the leading men of the "Essays and Reviews" hold, that it is a place of purification, of temporary duration. It appears to me altogether otherwise. But on this I do not dwell here. He says, My brethren are likely to be lost, just as I am. I want you, father Abraham, to send this poor man, Lazarus, to whom I cared not to give the crumbs that fell from my table, whose sores the dogs licked; I now see that he is in glory, he is happy; I am tormented; do send him, that he may speak a word to my five brethren, that they come not into this place of torment. He did not say, Send me, as if he felt that were hopeless, but send at least Lazarus. What was the answer? "They have Moses and the prophets." An attestation to the fullness, the sufficiency, and clearness of the Word of God not to be explained away. "They have Moses and the prophets." But he said, Nay, father Abraham; if one were to descend from the heights of heaven, radiant with its imperishable splendor, or if one were to emerge from the depths of hell, clad in its indescribable blackness, and were to tell them of the joys of the one, and of the miseries and the agonies of the other, they certainly could not withstand the appeal — they would inevitably repent. This was a momentous request, apparently most natural, feasible, and likely to succeed, if granted. But what is the answer? The rich man says, "They will repent." The answer of Abraham is, "If they hear not Moses and the prophets, neither will they be persuaded," not only will not repent, but they will not even be persuaded, "though one were to rise from the dead." But what does this answer teach us? Unquestionably that these writings which the Bishop of Natal says are impostures or fables of no authenticity or divine origin, are able to make wise unto salvation. Certainly the voice from heaven contradicts in the most emphatic terms the voice from Natal; for it tells us, that if a man is not saved by reading the way to be saved in the Pentateuch, he would not be saved if one were to come down from heaven, or to come up from hell, and preach to him the terrors of the one, or the glories and attractions of the other. What does this imply? That the Pentateuch, "Moses, and the prophets," contain as full, if not as clear, revelation of the way to heaven as the New Testament. What did these five need to learn? They wanted to be taught that time has its echoes in eternity, and its issues also; that acts in this world are reproduced in retributions in the world that is to come; that sin in this world unvisited on earth, is visited in the world to come; that a way of escape was needed; that a Saviour, in whose blood atonement would be found, was accessible. Let one, therefore, rise from the dead and tell them of these things. Nay, says Abraham, Moses tells them all these things. He has told them of a future; he has described the law of retribution; he has warned them of death, and judgment, and eternity; and if they see not these things to be true and solemn realities as they are portrayed in all their just proportions in the pages of the Pentateuch, then they will not see them more clearly, nor one whit more be persuaded of them if one were to rise from the dead and repeat them. Now, I ask you, as reasonable men, is it possible that there can be a higher attestation to the fullness and the sufficiency of the Mosaic record than what is contained in the language of Abraham; and the language of Abraham, mark you, attested and accepted by the Son of God? But is it true that Moses teaches these truths? I answer, Unquestionably so. Some persons have objected to Moses on this ground, that he does not teach immortality, that he does not speak often, if at all, of the immortality of the soul. Neither does the New Testament. In the same manner, and for the same reason, neither the Old nor the New Testament talk often of the existence of a God; they assume a God as the key-note of the harmonies of the universe. Nor do they speak often of the immortality of the soul; they assume the immortality of the soul as of the very essence of human being. In fact, there scarcely ever has been a nation or a pagan from the earliest to the latest times that has not believed in a God of some sort, and in an after existence, laden with everlasting retributions, of good or evil. But it has been urged that the rewards in the Mosaic record chiefly relate to time. I admit it. But what was the Jewish Church? A theocracy — a government by God Himself. The punishments were temporal, and visible; the rewards were temporal also; but it was equally the evidence and the lesson of retribution; and retribution existing in the limited scale of time is the foreshadow, and the earnest, and the pledge of retribution existing in eternity. What is providence? Retribution; God rewarding the good, God punishing the evil. And if Moses taught the great doctrine of retribution, or rewards and punishments, he taught the great truth that men needed to know, that it shall be well with the righteous, and that sin is the ruin of individuals, as it is the shame of nations. The Saviour Himself asserts that Moses taught these things, when He says, referring to the resurrection of the dead, "Have ye not read that which was spoken unto you by God; I am the God of Abraham, and the God of Isaac, and the God of Jacob? God is not the God of the dead, but the God of the living." Here, then, is the attestation of Abraham, accepted and confirmed by the Blessed Saviour, that the Mosaic record teaches punishments, the issues of sin; rewards, the fruits of holiness; an atonement through the blood of sprinkling, the way to enjoy the one, and to escape the other; and all the substantial and vital truths that are more fully and splendidly declared in the New

Testament were more dimly, but not less divinely, enunciated in the Pentateuch, or the books of Moses.

But after Abraham had told the rich man this, the rich man was not satisfied. "Nay, father Abraham;" as much as to say, that is not enough. I had Moses and the prophets, but I am now in hell. And therefore his argument was that Moses and the prophets were not sufficient. In other words, he regarded the writings of Moses and the prophets as altogether unreliable, unhistorical; in fact, he was Bishop Colenso, without the light and responsibility of the Bishop of Natal, but he was where restoration, and repentance, and recovery were altogether impossible. He wanted a better guide than Moses; whether it was the inner light that the Bishop insists on, or the outer light that others require; he was quite satisfied in hell that the Pentateuch was not historical, that its truths were not reliable. In the words of Bengel, the most eminent, and able, and impressive commentator on the New Testament, "Vilipendium scripturæ miser, relicto luxu secum intulit in inferno." "This contempt of Scripture the wretched man, after leaving his luxury behind, carried with him into hell." Moral character survives the grave. The contempt of Moses as insufficient, unhistorical, unreliable, we find in Natal; what a strange coïncidence! we find it in hell also. In heaven, admiration of Moses and the prophets; in hell, contempt of Moses and the prophets; in Scripture, and in the words of our Saviour, admiration and appreciation. The language of the lost man was, I want a brighter light than Moses can supply, kindled, if you like, in hell, and sent from beneath to warn my brethren not to come to this place of torment. The answer of Abraham is, They have a bright light, kindled in heaven, sent down from glory; and if they are not guided and enlightened by it they would not be enlightened nor instructed if one were to rise from the dead. The words are extremely emphatic. He says, But they would *repent* if one were to rise from the dead. The language of Abraham is, They would not even be *persuaded.* If they have obstinacy sufficient to shut their eyes upon the light that streams from the Pentateuch and the prophets, they won't open their eyes to receive and be convinced by the light that will stream from Him who will rise from the dead.

Can we have a more impressive or emphatic testimonial to Moses, than the voice of Abraham in heaven confirmed by the voice of the Son of God? Moses was the morning star that intimated the approach of the rising Sun of Righteousness. The Pentateuch was the soft, the beautiful, but true dawn that intimated and prophesied the approaching everlasting and glorious noon.

How conclusive an answer to those that say, Show us a sign. How many Christians, professing Christians, do we meet with, who say, Well, the Bible is all very good, and all very true; there is much in it that we like, much in it that we admire; but the truth is, we want God Almighty to show us some miraculous sign from heaven to strengthen our belief. Suppose God were to grant what you ask; suppose a spirit were to descend from heaven, wrapt in its intense and beautiful glory; or suppose a spirit were to come up from the vasty deep, clothed in the awful and intolerable shadow of death, suppose the one were to speak of the splendor of his inheritance, and the other of the torments no water can cool; what would be the effect? I know what hundreds say. Then we should no longer doubt Christianity, nor disbelieve the Bible, nor live a life of sin, of profligacy, and of unbelief. You are utterly mistaken; for after you had seen the vision you would consult your physician about your nerves; you would say, I have been greatly annoyed, my system must be unstrung and shattered. I have seen a very awful vision, and I know not what to make of it. How do you account for it? The doctor would instantly suggest, You have eaten something that has disagreed with you, and your nerves have in consequence become disturbed; your vision is cerebral and subjective, a mere *delusio visus;* it was nothing else. But it seemed so real that you would not be satisfied with such a solution. Next day you would read a great deal on the history of visions and specters, and perhaps you would say, Ah! it must have been a delusion. And the third day you would come to the conclusion that it was a dream, and nothing more; you would not believe it to be historical and real. So clear, so cogent, so full of all that man's mind needs, and that man's heart yearns for, is this blessed book, that no supernatural apparition, no voice from heaven or from hell, no revelation by pretended emissaries of a higher power, would have the least effect in convincing that man whom the Bible has failed to convince. For what is the constitution of man? He is not a creature to be terrified out of hell; or to be cajoled and charmed into heaven; he is a creature to be convinced in his intellect, to be enchained by his heart, to be persuaded through the truth brought home to his conscience, and heart, and intellect, just as we have it in the Word of God.

The whole drift of the prelate, to whom I have so frequently referred, is to make the Zulu believe that he is more enlightened than Moses, and the African tribes than the tribes of Israel, and to dissuade them from believing what Moses and the prophets teach, and to wait for what they never will find till the judgment overtakes the world—an emissary from the heavens above, or an emigrant from hell below, to persuade them to repent and accept the truth.

Abraham teaches here, and his words imply, and the Saviour authenticates them, that the Bible in the days of the apostles was in the hands of the laity. Who were the five brethren? Five men of the world, men of business; and "they have," he says, "Moses and the prophets." Well then, it does seem to me that if Moses and the prophets were fit to be put into the hands of the laity then, they can not be unsuitable to be read by the laity now. In other words, it is evidence that Protestantism is not the creation of the sixteenth century, but is as old as the religion of Moses, as the days of the apostles, and of our blessed Lord and Saviour Jesus Christ.

We are driven irresistibly to the conclusion that the Bishop has not read his Bible, or if he has, that he has read it through spectacles which have been extremely tinged and colored, or sadly perverting as a medium through which to understand it; and that the words of Moses are not the words of man, but the words of God; and that the statements of the Bishop of Natal are the unhappy crotchets of a deluded and an uninstructed mind.

I exceedingly rejoice to hear that the Jews, as a body, have been so startled by this attack made upon their Scriptures that thousands of them, I am credibly informed, are reading the Pentateuch who have had no time (for there are formal Jews just as there are formal Christians) to read it before. And it is a most gratifying thing that the most effective reply on certain points to the objections of the Bishop of Natal has been made by the Chief Rabbi of London. What a startling fact! how should it shake the confidence of the Bishop of Natal in his conclusion, that a Jewish rabbi has to defend the Word of God against a Christian Bishop! And yet, alas! if Dr. Colenso were alone, one would not mind it; but he is only one of the pickets of an advancing army; the more advanced of a host that take up the same sentiments. One of the writers of the "Essays and Reviews," Mr. Williams, who, instead of being turned out of his benefice, and sent to join a communion where such things may be preached with impunity, by the judgment pronounced upon him is to be one year suspended from his benefice, and lose the fruits of it—as if he cared one halfpenny for a judgment of that sort—instead of being expelled from a Church, which, in its Articles and its Liturgy, is most Scriptural; he is merely suspended for a year, and fined the product of his benefice, which can not be above a couple of hundred pounds, for that time. These essayists are, and have been, the teachers of the leading dogmas which, under the incubation of the Bishop of Natal, have developed themselves into the portentous heresies contained in this book.

But now, having said so much of these, let me proceed one step further, and show you that if the writers of the "Essays and Reviews" and the Bishop of Natal have so sorrowful and depreciatory an estimate and appreciation of the Word of God, the most illustrious of former days have formed a very different conclusion. I have been collecting for a good time the testimonies of the great and good to the integrity, the purity, and the excellence of the Word of God; and some of these I here present. One remarkable testimony is wrung from a skeptic, a sensual skeptic, Rousseau. He says, "This divine book needs only to be read with reflection to inspire love for its author, and most of all an ardent desire to obey its precepts. No one can rise from its perusal without feeling himself better than he was before. It is impossible that a book so simple and so sublime can merely be the work of man." And yet he lived a sensualist, he died a skeptic—a striking testimony to what a nobleman once said: "The only objection that is fatal to the Bible, that I know, is a bad heart." Let me quote, again, the testimony of a most illustrious personage, skilled in law, in logic, in literature, Sir Matthew Hale. He says, "I have been acquainted with men and books; I have had long experience in learning, and in the world. There is no book like the Bible for excellent learning, wisdom, and purity; and it is want of understanding in them who think or speak otherwise." A most accomplished person, who wrote much, and whose judgment was much relied on, the Hon. Robert Boyle, thus expressed himself: "The Bible, that matchless book. It is impossible we can study it too much, or esteem it too highly." John Locke, the founder of the deepest metaphysical philosophy, the man who did for the human mind what Sir Isaac Newton did for the stars and the universe, says, "Study the Holy Scriptures, especially the New Testament. Therein are contained the words of eternal life. This book has God for its author, salvation for its end, and truth without any mixture of error for its matter." Then John Milton, the noblest poet, who sung the days of Paradise in its glory, and Paradise in its ruins, and Paradise Regained, says, "There are no songs comparable to the songs of Zion; no orations equal to those of the prophets, no politics like those which the Scriptures teach." Dr. Samuel Johnson, one of the great classic authorities and writers of our language, on his death-bed, addressed a young man in these memorable words: "Young man, attend to the advice of one who has possessed some degree of fame in the world, and who will shortly appear before his Maker; read the Bible every day of your life." Again, Sir William Jones, the greatest linguist of his day, and whose name is celebrated for all that is profound, and illustrious, and good, wrote on the last leaf of his Bible, "I have regularly and attentively read the Holy Scriptures, and am of opinion that this volume, independently of its Divine origin, contains more sublimity and beauty, more pure morality, more important history of men, in strains of poetry and eloquence, than can be collected from all other books, of whatever age or in whatever language they be composed." And Lord Bacon, the founder of modern philosophy, the author of inductive science, thus writes upon it: "Thy works, O Lord, have been my book, but thy Scripture much more. I have sought thee in the country, I have sought thee in courts, in fields, and in the garden; but I have found thee in thy sanctuary, and in thy word." Sir Isaac Newton, who cast his line over the stars, who weighed them in scales, who estimated their density, calculated their distances, and was the profoundest and most illustrious scholar of ancient or of modern times, that great and gifted man says, "We account the Scriptures the most sublime philosophy." Bishop Colenso says that a little knowledge of geology makes him deny the Scriptures. Sir Isaac Newton says, "The Scriptures contain the most profound philosophy." The great Selden said, "There is no book on which we can rely in a dying hour, except the Bible." Dr. Mason Good, eminent and illustrious in his day, said, "Such a book is now in our hands; let us prize it, for it must be the word of God, as it bears the direct stamp and testimony of his works." Fisher Ames, the eminent American orator, says, "Should not the Bible regain the place it once held in the schoolroom? Its morals are pure, its examples captivating and noble." Professor Dana, a living and eminent American geologist, says, "The two records, the creation, the revelation, the earlier and the later, are one in their sublime enunciation of the history of creation; there is equal grandeur in the progress of the ages. They both contain conceptions infinitely beyond the reach of the human intellect, and bear equal evidence of their Divine origin." Wilberforce, the father of the present Bishop of Oxford, and the eminent advocate of the emancipation of the slave, gave this as his last testimony, "Read the Bible, read the Bible. Let no religious book take its place. Through all my perplexities and distresses I never read any other book. I never knew the want of any other. It has been my hourly study. Books about religion may be useful enough, but they will not do instead of the simple truth of the Bible." And Mr. Cecil, a predecessor of the Rev. Mr. Noel, in St. John's Chapel, in London, says: "This book resembles an extensive garden, where there is a vast variety of fruits and flowers, some more essential, some more splendid than others; but not a blade is suffered to grow that has not its use and beauty in the system." And, lastly, that marvelous man, whose life by Canon Stanley is the most interesting biography that was ever written, and worthy of being read a second and a third time, Dr. Arnold of Rugby, left this as his testimony: "A man's love of Scripture at the beginning of his religious life, is such as makes the praise of it which other Christians give to the Bible seem exaggerated; but after twenty or thirty years of religious life and experience, such praise always sounds inadequate; its glories seem so much more full then than they seemed at first."

Well now, put against these splendid testimonies the protest of the Bishop of Natal. Men competent for genius, experience, and knowledge of science have pronounced the Scriptures to be worthy of what is imputed to them, that God inspired them, and that holy men inspired by Him wrote them.

How just is the Divine account of Scripture: "The words of the Lord are pure words; as silver tried in a furnace of earth, purified seven times." The Bishop says there is an alloy in them; that instead of being seventeen or twenty carats fine, they are not above three or four carats fine; that the alloy preponderates, that the dross exceeds the silver, and some parts are only electro-plated, a thin coating of silver that disguises the large amount of worthless brass that is beneath. But God says very differently; they are words tried as silver; the dross consumed, the alloy eliminated, and the evidence irresistible to every one that candidly inquires, "Thy word, O God, is truth."

It is a heavy charge to make against a Christian Bishop, that he has attempted in his printed works to undermine the authority and limit the claims of the Word of God. The Bible is the depository of the hopes of millions—their rule of life and faith—and whatever touches it touches the ark of God. But this heavy charge has been proved in these Lectures to the satisfaction of every thoughtful mind that has heard or read them. Were I alone in making this grave assertion it would still rest on its only right foundation—the extracts and evidence adduced—evidence accessible and intelligible to the humblest reader. But with a unanimity almost unprecedented, the chief ministers of the Church of England have pronounced judgment in terms even stronger and more decided than those employed in these Lectures.

Among these one whose sound judgment, consistent piety, and thorough acquaintance with the merits of this subject it is impossible to doubt, gave forth a well-considered estimate of their character and destructive tendencies at a meeting of the Scripture Readers' Society, recently held at Leeds. The Bishop of Ripon, who occupied the chair, spoke as follows :—

"He said it was particularly painful to find a man in high office in the Church miserably perverting his talents, so as to employ them, not for the advancement of Divine truth, but rather in disparagement of the claims of the inspired Word of God. For his own part, painful as that spectacle was, he (the Bishop of Ripon) did not anticipate that any very great evil would result from the attempt to which he had referred. The objections which had been brought forward against the historical accuracy of the Pentateuch were very old and threadbare: there was nothing new in them. Nor was it difficult to perceive how easily these objections might be disposed of by those who had their minds firmly rooted in the persuasion that the Bible was the inspired Word of God. Let it be borne in mind what the conclusion really was, supposing they took Dr. Colenso's views to be accurate. If this view is a just one, then we may suppose the Pentateuch to be the production of a very clever impostor. If an impostor, the writer of the Pentateuch must have been an exceedingly clever one. But was it to be supposed for one moment that, being such a clever impostor, he would have allowed such palpable absurdities as — if they believed the Bishop to be right — existed in the book? The very openness of the Pentateuch, the matters which lie on the surface of the book, and which Dr. Colenso would have us take as a sufficient ground for doubt—were in themselves a sufficient answer to the objections which had been raised on the point of historical accuracy. They must also bear this in mind, that every part of the Bible is so interwoven with the other parts, that to invalidate any one portion was to throw discredit upon the rest, so that if you undermined the authority of the Pentateuch, you would also invalidate the authority of the Prophets, of the historical portions of the Bible, and of the New Testament. Each part so intertwines with the rest that to throw discredit upon one portion was to throw discredit upon the whole. If they could successfully disprove the historical accuracy of the Pentateuch, they would scarcely have any thing left in the Bible on which the mind could lay hold for peace and comfort, as truth to be relied upon, as truth saving in its nature."

CHAPTER X.

THE STONES OF EGYPT WITNESSES TO MOSES.

THERE is another line of witnesses to Moses. This is traced on the monumental stones and hieroglyphic writings of Egypt. I may therefore say, "If Moses should hold his peace, the stones would immediately cry out."

This subject is one of great and peculiar interest. The scope and object of all that I shall now adduce will be to show that if the Mosaic record can not be accepted as historical by clear spiritual proofs, such as I have adduced on previous occasions, and as a genuine and authentic document, we can demonstrate from the monuments of ancient Egypt, and from the remains of its tombs, and with clear and irresistible force, that if all the evangelists, and apostles, and prophets were to hold their tongues, the stones of Egypt still open their mouths and speak out. To those that ask for this evidence I will explain its origin in few, and, I hope, plain and intelligible words.

We find in ancient times, and at periods demonstrably contemporaneous with those in which the events recorded in Genesis and in Exodus took place, that it was the habit of the ancient Egyptians to trace upon stones, and monuments, and tombs, inscriptions or records of events that had taken place, and of the characters, biographies, exploits, and histories of illustrious men. It was a universal practice for the Egyptians to inscribe upon the monuments and tombs of those that slept in them the records of events they were historically associated with. We find inscriptions traced on the stones showing what were the living dynasties, who the living kings, and what events transpired in their reigns.

I have here a work written by Hengstenberg, one of the most learned and eminent of continental writers, who has collected, in brief space, the most remarkable inscriptions on the tombs and obelisks; also the work of Osburn, a very able writer, who has likewise given sketches and drawings of these monuments and stones, containing records of events associated with the Israelites; also a most excellent *resumé* of the magnificent work of Lepsius by Rev. B. Saville. I proceed to give you some facts discovered by these and other learned men, which will show more forcibly than any argument of mine could do, that Moses, the inspired penman, is invariably right, and that Dr. Colenso is not only wrong, but has made the most rash and unwarrantable assertions.

First of all, ancient historians give the name of Menes, or Mizraim, the Scripture name, as that of the first man who reigned in Egypt. The Scripture date is 100 years after the Flood, at which time the dispersion occurred, upward of 2,000 years before the birth of

Christ. This very name is found at the *top* of the list of ancestors of Rameses Sesostris, in a relief of a royal palace near Gournou, in Western Thebes. It is also found in the Turin papyrus brought from Thebes. Champollion says:—

> I have demonstrated that no Egyptian monument is older than the year 2,200 before the Christian era. This certainly is high antiquity, but it presents nothing contradictory to the sacred histories. I venture to affirm it establishes them on all points; for it is a fact, by adopting the chronology and succession of kings given by the Egyptian monuments that the Egyptian history wonderfully accords with the sacred writings.

Let me notice another striking coïncidence—and these things speak for themselves, they require no comment. Moses relates that Abraham went down into Egypt, and that the reigning Pharaoh gave him "sheep, and oxen, and he asses, and menservants, and maidservants, and she asses, and camels." Josephus says:—

> Abraham taught the Egyptians the science of astronomy.

Osburn, in his Monumental History of Egypt says:—

> It is a well-established synchronism of much value that Abraham went into Egypt in the reign of Pharaoh Acthoes.

There is no evidence of any Egyptian king before him. But on the monuments there is evidence that the son and successor of this Pharaoh had learned astronomy, such as it was then known.

Again, we can demonstrate from the monuments this

fact, that a certain Pharaoh, of a certain dynasty, reigned in Egypt when Joseph was carried into Egypt as a slave. His name was Apophis, or Pheops. We can demonstrate with a force that would satisfy even Bishop Colenso that, under the reign of that Pharaoh, a person, named Joseph—his name Eitsuph, inscribed upon the stones still remaining in the land of Egypt—was selected by Pharaoh to be the distributor of grain—the saviour of his country. The sojourning of the children of Israel in Egypt was 430 years from the call of Abraham, and 215 years from the descent of Jacob into Egypt to the Exode. Well, a tomb was discovered in recent researches in Egypt, and on this tomb is written, translated from the hieroglyphic into English, the name Eitsuph, that is, Joseph. On deciphering the inscriptions on this tomb we find him spoken of as one who had been introduced into the land; who had been raised to be what he is called in Scripture, the saviour of his country; who had been elevated by the reigning Pharaoh to be the distributor and guardian of the granaries of the land. Compare the coïncidence, which is so remarkable, between the Scripture records of Joseph and the inscriptions on the monuments, and the dynasty that was reigning when Joseph was appointed; and if Dr. Colenso will not believe the history that is recorded in Moses, he must be driven to accept the history recorded on the stones. So that if Moses were silent, the stones would open their eloquent lips, and declare that the record of the

Pentateuch is true. We learn, as already stated, from the inscriptions on the Egyptian monuments, that the Pharaoh reigning in Egypt when Joseph was carried there as a slave, was Apophis or Pheops. He was the patron of Joseph. When Joseph was invested with power, it is said, "Pharaoh called his name Zaphnath-paaneah, and he gave him to wife Asenath, the daughter of Potipherah, priest of On." The name given to Joseph is rendered in the margin of our Bible, "a revealer of secrets." Rosellini interprets it, "Saviour of the age." Gesenius, "Sustainer of the age." Osburn, "One with Neith, the goddess of wisdom." This last is justified by Pharaoh's address to Joseph; "None so discreet and wise as thou." His wife's name, "She who sees Neith," goddess of wisdom. Mr. Saville, in his able work, states:—

At Beull Hasan, on the Nile, about 100 miles north of Thebes, there has been discovered the tomb of Nevotp, an officer of high rank under Sesertesen II. On this tomb there is a representation of an occurrence in the sixth year of that monarch, in which two Egyptians are presenting to their master a party of strangers, consisting of ten males, four females, with two children on a donkey, and a lad bearing a spear. The inscription calls them, "The great foreign prisoners." No one who has seen the magnificent work of Lepsius, in which the paintings on Egyptian monuments are copied with extreme fidelity, can for a moment doubt that these strangers bear in their features the strongly marked characteristics of the Jewish race. When, moreover, we find that Sesertesen II. was ruling at Thebes when Pharaoh Apophis was at the commencement of his long reign, we think this remarkable painting must refer to the arrival of the family of Jacob in Egypt. Though called prisoners, they are not represented in the guise of prisoners, but armed and at liberty, which would seem to intimate they were an honorary deputation from Lower Egypt to an officer of the rival dynasty in the Upper country, during an interval in the civil war.

Again, in Genesis xlvii. 20, we read —

And Joseph bought all the land of Egypt for Pharaoh; for the Egyptians sold every man his field, because the famine prevailed over them; so the land became Pharaoh's. Only the land of the priests bought he not.

This refers to the seven years' famine, and the people selling their land for food. Osburn says —

The monumental proofs of the occurrence of this modification in the social condition of Egypt are just as striking as any of those which have engaged us. The tombs of the eras that follow that of Apophis bear unequivocal testimony to a great political change having taken place in the condition of the inhabitants of Egypt at this period. In old Egypt scarcely an act of any Pharaoh is recorded on the tombs of his subjects. Nor does his name appear save in the names of their estates. But in the tombs of the new kingdom, or that of the times that followed Joseph, all this is reversed. There is scarcely a tomb of any importance, the principal subject of which is not some act of service or devotion by the excavator to the reigning family. The cause of this change we plainly discover in the legislation of Joseph.

This writer then proceeds to show that the priesthood, after the days of Joseph, was raised to new dignity and power, arising from the forbearance of the king to exact payment for corn supplied to the temple. On the Rosetta Stone there is this inscription :

"Ptolemy Epiphanes ordered that the revenues of the temple and the annual contributions to them in corn and money should remain every where as usual." Here are effects indicating an origin which is found in the history of Joseph in Egypt, as written in the Scriptures.

But, you say, how can the tomb of Joseph be in Egypt, when we know from Scripture that his bones, according to his own directions, were carried into the land of Canaan? The answer is, Joseph died 144 years before the Exode from Egypt into Canaan. We read in Genesis, "And Joseph said unto his brethren, I die; and God will surely visit you, and bring you out of this land unto the land which He sware to Abraham, to Isaac, and to Jacob. And Joseph took an oath of the children of Israel, saying, God will surely visit you, and ye shall carry up my bones from hence. So Joseph died, being an hundred and ten years old; and they embalmed him, and he was put in a coffin in Egypt." Now, it was the practice of the Egyptians to build their monuments before they died; and for this great man, described on the monuments as the saviour of his country, as the head of the granaries, a tomb of unrivaled magnificence and beauty, was built; and there his dead dust lay for 144 years, till the night when the firstborn of Egypt were slain, and it was carried by the faithful Israelites into the land which God had promised, and where Joseph expressed his desire that it should be carried at that time. And thus we demonstrate the truth of the history of Joseph;

for the leading links of his biography are traceable there, and distinctly so. I here quote another extract from Mr. Saville's work, to prove what I have stated. He says:

> There are still in existence at Sakkara, opposite Memphis, in Lower Egypt, the ruins of the tomb of a distinguished personage, whose name in hieroglyphics accords with that of Joseph. It is close in the vicinity of the largest pyramid, of the group which Osburn considers to have been the tomb of Apophis. On the relief of the tomb referred to, the names and titles of Joseph appear in great beauty. The name is written in hieroglyphics, *Ei tsuph*—"he came to save." The title under which Joseph's power was inaugurated, as we read in the Book of Genesis, by the people crying Abrech, "Bow the knee," appears likewise on the tomb. He is also called Director of the Granaries of the Chiefs of both Egypts.

If the Bishop of Natal refuses the history of Moses, let him hear a voice rising from the tombs of Egypt attesting Moses right and the Bishop of Natal wrong.

We turn to another incident of the very same kind, and a no less remarkable one. We find the name of the Pharaoh that reigned in Egypt at the time that the Exode or Exodus was about to take place. That Pharaoh's name is contained on the monuments, and can be identified also from Scripture. We find inscribed upon the monuments the record that this last Pharaoh had a most troublesome, disturbed, and revolutionary reign; that his later history was a scene of perplexity and trouble. His name was Tuthmosis IV. Osburn says that at this period there are signs of troublous times in Egypt, and "indications that Tuthmosis IV.

had a turbulent reign." And we should naturally expect that the Pharaoh at the time of the exode would have a troubled reign. We find one account of his reign, contained on one of the monuments, the Great Sphinx at Ghizeh, describes first his character, next his exploits, next the long line of his predecessors, and it adds, "And then;" and there it stops. We know nothing more of him. We find he was the reigning Pharaoh when Moses led the Israelites out of Egypt into the desert; we find on the monuments evidence irresistible that he was so; we find the description that identifies him with the Pharaoh of the Exode; but that after all that is good and great has been spoken of him, it suddenly breaks off with, "And then;" after which all is blank. But this strange and silent blank is more than striking eloquence. We find that Pharaoh's tomb is not to be discovered in Egypt; the tombs of the previous Pharaohs are all found and identified; but his is wanting. What is the obvious inference? That he was the Pharaoh that pursued the Israelites with his brilliant horsemen into the desert, and that he perished in the Red Sea, over which Miriam and Moses stood, and praised Him who had triumphed gloriously.

Let me notice another coïncidence. No language can over-estimate the value of these facts in connection with Dr. Colenso's objections. For a long time Egypt was an absolute mystery, impenetrable to archæologists and travelers. But, as the world would call it, accidentally—as we know, in the providence of God—a stone was found in Egypt called the Rosetta Stone, to which I have already alluded. On one portion of this stone were the usual hieroglyphic characters, giving certain records and accounts; on a second portion of it was the demotic character, or the character used in the language of the people, translating this; and on a third portion of it was a translation of it into the Greek language. The instant that Champollion and Young discovered this last fact, they found the key to the interpretation of all the records on the monuments of Egypt, and by that key they are able now to read those mysterious hieroglyphs almost as easily as a scholar can read a chapter in Hebrew or in Greek, and to affix and perpetuate their translated meaning. We find another fact most remarkably confirmatory of what I have been asserting,—the historic truth of the Exode and the Mosaic record. It is this. We ascertain the king who reigned at the time of the Exode; his name is given, his character perfectly identified. We find on the monuments the hieroglyphic picture of the queen, this Pharaoh's wife, having recently given birth to a child, that child a son. Two handmaids are represented chafing her hands, as if she were in sorrow, or in fear, or in peril; and another handmaiden is represented, holding the son up before her, as if saying, "Rejoice that a man child and an heir to the throne is born." The chronology of the monuments and the chronology of Scripture being here perfectly parallel, we discover that the successor to that Pharaoh whose son was then born turns out not to be his eldest, but his second son; and the record simply states that he had an elder son, of whose life and death nothing is said, and that he was succeeded by a younger son; and this birth occurred about that very night when the angel of death went forth and killed every one of the firstborn, from the son of Pharaoh on the throne down to the son of the meanest of his subjects. Now, what is the highly probable inference from this? That if the Scriptures hold their tongue, the stones, and rocks, and monuments of Egypt cry out; and that, therefore, if Dr. Colenso believes that Moses is not to be trusted as an honest, impartial, and reliable historian, he has only to take the work of Osburn, or Hengstenberg, or Wilkinson, or Taylor, or Rev. B. Saville, or (and having gone to Natal, he surely can accomplish the voyage to Egypt), to visit Egypt, and there, if he will shut the mouth of Moses, he will hear the stones crying out, "Thy word, O God, is truth."

I might multiply these evidences still more, and in doing so, I should only continue to confirm and further to illustrate what I have already stated, that the whole monumental history of Egypt runs parallel with the whole Mosaic record in the Pentateuch; and that, therefore, the statement of Dr. Colenso, which he has reïterated, with awful exaggerations, in his second volume, recently published, that Moses is not a true historian, is confuted, and completely destroyed, by finding a history parallel and cotemporaneous with it, by writers who used the chisel, and the stony rock, and the mummy case, on which they wrote their story, who had no interest in the Old Testament Scriptures, who disbelieved, if they ever were offered, the knowledge of the Gospel of Christ; whose testimony, therefore, unswayed by prejudice, and unswerving from any possibly false or spurious motive, must be accepted as a faithful, impartial, and historic record. And perhaps when Dr. Colenso learns that, he may come to the extravagant conclusion, that somebody else must have written the Pentateuch; some Egyptian priest; at all events he can not deny the facts that the stones so eloquently proclaim, and which are substantially the facts recorded in the Pentateuch.

Here let me give another interesting fact as quoted by Mr. Saville:—

At Gournou, near Thebes, there is still standing the tomb of one of the nobles. The owner of this tomb bears the name of Roshera, which signifies, "A prince like the sun!" The paintings of this tomb, which are given with great fidelity in Lepsius's magnificent work, afford indisputable proof not only of the Israelites being in Egypt at this period of history, but of being forcibly engaged in the very occupation to which Scripture informs us they were compelled by the jealousy of the Pharaohs of that dynasty which knew not Joseph. One inscription, "The reception of the tribute of the land brought to the king by the captives in person." On another, "The bringing in of the offerings of the unclean races." These prisoners wear *torn* garments, are engaged in *making bricks*, and carefully watched by Egyptian taskmasters.

In Hengstenberg, you will find in his description of the various scenes and incidents spoken of by Moses, how thoroughly exact and historically accurate is the Mosaic record. Take this one. According to Exodus i. 14, Pharaoh embittered the life of the Israelites "with hard bondage, in mortar, and in brick." We find, from other remains, that it was the custom of the Israelites in that day rarely to burn the bricks, and generally to harden them in the hot sunshine; and in order to give the bricks cohesiveness, straw was mixed up with the clay. Hengstenberg says:—

Bricks were made in Egypt under the direction of the king or some privileged person, as appears from the impressions found upon many of them. A great multitude of strangers were constantly employed in the brick-fields of Thebes and other parts of Egypt. But the most remarkable agreement with the Pentateuch is in the fact, that *a small portion of chopped straw* is found in the composition of the Egyptian bricks. This is evident from an examination of those brought by Rosellini from Thebes, on which is the stamp of Thothmes IV., the fifth king of the eighteenth dynasty. "The bricks," remarks Rosellini, "which are now found in Egypt, belonging to the same period, always have straw mingled with them, although in some of those that are most carefully made, it is found in very small quantities." According to Rosellini, straw was used in order that the bricks, (they were not for the most part burned, but dried in the sun,) might be more firm, especially those of coarse clay and more roughly formed. Prokesch says, "The bricks (of the first pyramid at Dashoor) are of fine clay from the Nile, mingled with chopped straw. This intermixture gives the bricks an astonishing durability." The *inquirer* will not leave unnoticed such little and entirely undesigned circumstances as these. We are carried much farther by the comparison of our history with a picture discovered in a tomb at Thebes, of which Rosellini first furnished a drawing and an explanation; "Explanation of a picture representing the Hebrews as they were engaged in making brick." We will first give an abstract of the account of Rosellini. "Of the laborers," says he, "some are employed in transporting the clay in vessels, some intermingling it with the straw; others are taking the bricks out of the form and placing them in rows; still others with a piece of wood upon their backs, and ropes on each side, carry away the bricks already burned or dried. Their dissimilarity to the Egyptians appears at the first view; the complexion, physiognomy, and beard permit us not to be mistaken in supposing them to be Hebrews. They wear at the hips the apron which is common among the Egyptians, and there is also represented as in use among them a kind of short trowsers. Among the Hebrews, four Egyptians, very distinguishable by their mien, figure, and color, are seen; two of them, one sitting and the other standing, carry a stick in their hand, ready to fall upon two other Egyptians, who are here represented like the Hebrews, one of them carrying on his shoulder a vessel of clay, and the other returning from the transportation of brick, carrying his empty vessel to get a new load. The tomb belonged to a high court officer of the king, Rochscerê, and was made in the time of Thothmes IV., the fifth king of the eighteenth dynasty." The question, "How came this picture in the tomb of Rochscerê?" Rosellini answers as follows:—"He was the overseer of the public buildings, and had, consequently, the charge of all the works undertaken by the king. There are found represented therein still other objects of a like nature; two colossal statues of kings, a sphinx and the laborers who hewed the stone, — works which he by virtue of his office had caused to be performed in his lifetime." To the question, "How came the representation of the labors of the Israelites at Thebes?" it is answered, "We need not suppose that the labors were performed in the very place where they are represented, for Rochscerê was overseer of the royal buildings throughout the land, and what was done in the circuit of his operations could, wherever performed, be represented in his tomb at Thebes. It is also not impossible that the Hebrews went even to Thebes. In Exodus v. 12, it is said that they scattered themselves through the whole land of Egypt in order to procure straw." So far Rosellini. The agreement of this painting, with our account in many very striking points, appears at first view. We consequently select from them only two. 1. It is said in the narrative, the Israelites were subjected to severe labor in mortar and brick. Just so this servile labor appears throughout the painting as twofold; some are employed upon the clay from which the bricks were made, and some upon the finished brick. 2. We have in this painting an explanation with regard to the Egyptians who accompanied the Israelites in their Exodus. Of these Egyptians we read, first, in Exodus xii. 38, "And also a great rabble went up with them." In Numbers xi. 4, "The mixed Egyptian populace led astray the Israelites in the desert to discontentment." In Deuteronomy xxix. 10, 11, let it be observed how accurately these remote and disconnected passages agree with each other; the Egyptian aliens appear as very poor, as the lowest servants, as hewers of wood and drawers of water. The designations *rabble* and *populace* in the first passages, also show that these attendants of the Israelites belonged to the lowest grades of society. Just such people we should naturally expect to find in Egypt. Their existence is the necessary consequence of strongly marked *castes* in society. The monuments indeed place vividly before us most manifest distinctions in station. A part of the people appear to be in the deep degradation which now presses upon the Fellahs. According to Herodotus, the caste of swineherds, a native tribe, was unclean and despised in Egypt. All intercourse with the rest of the inhabitants, even entrance into a temple, was forbidden, and they were as much despised as the Pariahs in India. The contempt in which they were held was not, certainly, the consequence of their occupation, but their occupation of the disdain which was felt for them. Already unclean, they had no reason for avoiding the care of unclean animals. But full light first falls upon these notices of the Pentateuch through our painting. We see upon it Egyptians who are placed entirely on an equality with the hated and despised foreigners. What is more natural than that a considerable part of these Egyptians, bound close to their companions in sorrow by their common misery, should leave with them their native land, such now to them only in name?

He who has carefully examined the engraving in Rosellini, the great importance of which has been acknowledged by such historians as Heeren, perceiving its striking accordance with the Pentateuch, will ask first of all, whether, then, this picture is really genuine, whether it is not probably a supposititious work, prepared after the Pentateuch was written. This question, almost sufficiently answered by the condition of the painting itself, is, by the judicious Wilkinson, who made a new examination on the spot, decided entirely in favor of the picture. This decision is the more to be relied on, since Wilkinson, while he questions whether the painting has direct reference to the labors of the Israelites, does not deny the significance of it for the Pentateuch. But the arguments with which he contends against its referring to Israelites are of so little importance, that we can scarcely avoid thinking that he is influenced by something foreign from the thing itself; and they are decidedly outweighed by the evident Jewish bearing and cast of physiognomy, which can be traced even in the common woodcuts, such as are found in Taylor.

Mark well this fact, which is so remarkable. I have seen only the engravings, or pictures. Every body knows what is the distinguishing and characteristic Jewish contour, or countenance, or face; it is so marked, so distinguishable, that nobody can possibly mistake it. Well, we find the Jewish face on all these monuments, perfectly marked, so that there can be no mistake that it is the countenance of the Jew, and the picture the representation of Jews who were engaged in that work. We also find on the monuments the negro, not employed in brick-making but in other work; and the negro, or African face, is equally marked and distinctive. Here is a painting, you observe, on an ancient monument, which shows the Israelites at the very period to which the chronology of the painting refers, engaged in the very work ascribed to them in Scripture; superintended, as I have noticed in the engraving, by hard taskmasters, each with a stick ready to smite the Hebrew that blunders in his work, or wearies in his hard and incessant drudgery: another evidence that has survived the lapse of centuries, and confirms, if confirmation were needed, the conclusion we have already come to, that the records of Moses are historically true, and reliable as facts.

Let me present another instance. We read constantly in the Mosaic record of the extreme arrogance of the Pharaohs. We find an illustration of this from the monuments.

"The insolent pride," says Hengstenberg, "with which Pharaoh received the message communicated by Moses, as, 'Who is Jehovah, that I should hear his voice, to let Israel go? I know not Jehovah, and will not let Israel go.' The obstinacy which he afterward exhibits, when the Divine punishments fall upon him one after another, in deciding to go to destruction with his land and people rather than yield, are all proved on the monuments in various ways, to be in accordance with the genuine spirit of a Pharaoh."

Now, just read the records of that memorable night when Pharaoh at last determined, out of desperation, in dread of utterly exterminating judgments, to let the children of Israel go; and you have a picture there of Pharaoh, just as reïterated and repeated on the monuments and in the paintings of Egypt.

"A comparison," continues Hengstenberg, "of the victory of Remeses Meiamun, in Thebes, explained by Champollion, is of special interest in this connection. The Pharaoh, it is there said, at whose feet they lay down these trophies of victory, (the severed right hand and other members of the body,) sits quietly in his chariot, while his horses are held by his officers, and directs a haughty speech to his warriors: 'Give yourselves to mirth; let it rise to heaven. Strangers are dashed to the ground by my power. Terror of my name has gone forth; their hearts are full of it; I appear before them as a lion; I have pursued them as a hawk; I have annihilated their wicked souls. I have passed over their rivers; I have set on fire their castles; I am to Egypt what the god Mandoo has been; I have vanquished the barbarians; Amun Ke, my father, subdued the whole world under my feet, and I am king on the throne forever.'"

Now this is the boasting language, copied from the monuments, that you find falling from the lips of Pharaoh in the Mosaic record.

And therefore the inevitable conclusion is, that these monuments justify the historial accuracy of Moses; as well as every touch, and sketch, and light, and shadow, on the countenances of the characters so vividly and so faithfully portrayed by the pen of the inspired historian.

Who can fail to see in all this, God storing up cumulative proofs of the historic purity and truthfulness of His Holy Word? Who can doubt that this blessed Word is under the guardian care of Him who sleepeth not, nor slumbereth? May its opponents be led to other and better thoughts.

It is important, in answer to the charge of Dr. Colenso, to show that from sources over which neither Jew nor Gentile had any control, we can advance the most conclusive evidences of the facts and events which Moses records. Were an unbaptized and uninstructed Zulu to be made acquainted with the method of interpreting the hieroglyphic inscriptions on the monuments of Egypt, and being ignorant of the Pentateuch, left in the midst of these remains to write out, from his study of these characters, a history of events, beginning 1,500 years before the Christian era, he would describe facts, and persons, and events so like those recorded in Genesis and Exodus, that Dr. Colenso, on reading them, would accuse him of plagiarism from the Pentateuch.

This field of illustration is of vast extent; extracts illustrative of the historic truth of the Mosaic record from the Egyptian monuments might be continued long enough to fatigue and weary the reader; but some are so conclusive for Moses and the strict historic truth of his writings in the Pentateuch, that no apology is needed for bringing forward at least the most important. A monument has been discovered in Egypt, the inscription on which indicates that it was written soon after the dispersion from the plains of Shinar, and that the group whom it represents were the very persons who were dispersed over the earth, in consequence of the confusion of tongues on that memorable, and really, and truly, historic occasion.

A singular verification (says Osburn, in his elaborate and beautiful work,) of the Scripture account of the dispersion of the descendants of Ham arises from these hieroglyphic names. Canaan, the first-born, who lost his birthright through his grandfather's curse (Gen. ix. 25, *seq.*,) and is therefore always placed last among his brethren (chap. x. 6, etc.), nevertheless seems to have been allowed the claims of seniority, when the sons of Ham together went forth to the westward from the plains of Shinar (Gen. xi.), and gave his name to the first district at which the emigrants would arrive. The descendants of Cush, the second son, took the next region to the westward, which consisted of the sterile sands of the deserts of Sinai. The fertile valley of the Nile was the happier lot of Misraim, the third son; while the descendants of Phut, the youngest, were driven forth to seek a comfortless home amid the trackless wastes of the Sahara. These names are all found on the monuments of Egypt (for, as we shall see hereafter, the hieroglyphic name of Canaan is still extant) with the exception of the name of Mizraim; which may, however, possibly be detected in that of the well-known demigod and hero of the Egyptian mythology, Osiris.

This is associated with some great event that led to the peopling of the heretofore uninhabited world. Here then is a monumental reference to the dispersion itself.

The same writer says:—

The pyramids of Ghizeh, in the burial-place of Memphis, are the most ancient of all the greater remains. Several of the tombs in their immediate vicinity also belong to the same remote period. As we proceed up the valley of the Nile to Beni Hassan and Abydos, the remains are those of the era of Osortasen; while at Thebes, and the regions to the south of it, we scarcely find a trace of any thing that is earlier than the eighteenth dynasty. More satisfactory proof could scarcely be desired that the progress of the first inhabitants of the valley was from Heliopolis upward; not from Thebes downward, as has been too hastily assumed by certain modern antiquaries. In this particular, therefore, the monuments of Egypt strongly confirm the Scripture account of the first dispersion of mankind from the plains of Shinar.

Another very important and interesting fact is narrated by this same writer. It relates to the names of the sons of Noah. He says:—

There is a design which is repeated in the tombs of the later kings of the eighteenth dynasty, and which evidently embodies the notions entertained by the Egyptians of the inhabitants of the earth. The most ancient copy of this design is in the tomb of Sethos I., which was discovered by Belzoni. The picture represents four individuals of four races of men, who are conducted, or rather directed, by the Divine hawk of the sun; denoted by the figure of an idol with a hawk's head. Its object is to show the superiority of Egypt over all other lands, through the blessing of her tutelary divinity, the sun—the first king of Egypt, from whom, as we have said, all his successors took their well-known title of Pharaoh, that is, *φρε*, "the sun." Immediately after the sun are four Egyptians, who are named "the human race," meaning, as will abundantly appear, that they were preëminently men above all other men. Above them is a hieroglyphic inscription, which reads as follows:—"The discourse of the hawk governing the appearance of the sun, in the third hororary mansion (*i. e.*, in the third hour of the day,) to the black land (Upper Egypt), and the red land (Lower Egypt). The sun, firm in his greatness in heaven, enlightens you, O ye kings (of the world). He vivifies the breath of your nostrils (whilè ye live); he dries your mummies (when ye are dead). Your eyes are dazzled by my brightness, O ye of the chief race of men."

The appearance of the race of men next in order varies considerably in costume and complexion in the several repetitions of this picture, which occur in the tombs of different kings; but all the copies agree in representing a people of much lighter complexion than the Egyptians, with blue eyes, and the hair inclining to red or flaxen, or, in some cases, black. We shall hereafter have the opportunity of identifying these races with the inhabitants of Canaan and of the regions to the eastward of that country. In the name which is common to them in all the copies of this picture we at once recognize the Shemites, the descendants of the patriarch Shem, who occupied the country immediately to the eastward of Canaan, and were confounded by the Egyptians with the inhabitants of that country: probably because they all spoke dialects of the same language. The inscription is, "The sun drives ye away, O ye who are named the Shemites.

The sun is unto you as the Divine vengeance, that he may afflict your souls. In my manifestation I have smitten them; I curse them in all the seasons that I shine (*i. e.*, at all times)."

The next tetrad of figures in this procession are negroes, who are called Nahasi, which we find elsewhere to have been a general appellation of all the dark races of mankind, or rather of the inhabitants of the regions to the south and west of Egypt. The dresses of these negroes vary in different copies, like the former group. The inscription reads, "O ye who are named the race of Nahasi, the sun (speaks unto) these; he takes vengeance on their souls; mine eye glistens upon them (in wrath)."

The fourth, and last group of this curious picture consists of four men, of a complexion much lighter than the Shemites, and resembling in appearance the Caucasian races. We shall find, hereafter, that by this group we are to understand the Hamathites, or ancient inhabitants of Syria, which being the farthest point to the north to which the geographical knowledge of the Egyptians extended, its name was adopted as a general appellation of all countries to the north of Canaan. The costumes, which vary like the rest, will be found described hereafter. The inscription in the tomb of Sethos, which is the only one that has been copied entire, is much mutilated. Enough of it, however, remains to show that the Hamathites were considered to inhabit merely a district in the region of which the Shemites were also inhabitants; for, like them, they are called there and in all other copies, "the great water." It seems probable that this is a reminiscence of the original settlement of the inhabitants of Egypt, on the banks of the Euphrates, from which they were expelled by the confusion of tongues. The epithet of the Euphrates, "the great river," which is universal to all ancient languages, appears to have been applied by them to those of the human race whom they left upon its banks, to distinguish them from the tribes who had set out in quest of new countries before the Egyptians.

These names point very intelligibly to the original and natural division of the human race into the descendants of the three sons of Noah. The Shemites retain the name of their progenitor; the Hamathites represented the Japhetians; while in the tribes already darkened by the burning sun of the tropics, who had first braved the terrors of the deserts to the south and west of Egypt, they recognized the sons of Ham. The vanity of the Egyptians, however, allowed to none of these races the slightest affinity with themselves. They were altogether of another and superior stock, which they erected into a fourth patriarchate at the head of the other three. It is pretty evident that the original genealogies of the several families of mankind had been forgotten in Egypt at the period of the monuments we are now considering. A vague recollection of the triple division of the human race, and the name of Shem seems to have been the extent of their knowledge of it.

I will now copy a very remarkable chapter from Hengstenberg, to whose work I have before referred, on the land of Goshen. He says:—

The references of the Pentateuch to the geographical features of Egypt, as we should naturally expect in a book of sacred history, are neither numerous nor particular, yet enough of these references exist to show that its author possessed an accurate knowledge of the topography of the country to which he alludes. And the more scattered, incidental, and undesigned these notices are, the more certain is the proof which they afford that the author's knowledge was of no secondary character, was not laboriously produced for the occasion; but on the contrary, natural, acquired from his own personal observation, and was such as to preserve him from every mistake, without the necessity of his being constantly on his guard.

Let us direct our attention, first, to what the author says of *the land of Goshen.* He nowhere gives a direct and minute account of the situation of this land. But it is evident that this must be referred to some other cause than his ignorance, since he communicates, in reference to it, a great number of separate circumstances which, although some of them appear at first view to be entirely at variance with each other, are yet found to be entirely consistent, when applied to a particular district.

The land of Goshen appears, *on the one hand*, as the eastern border-land of Egypt. Thus it is said, Gen. xlvi. 28: "And he (Jacob) sent Judah before him unto Joseph, to direct his face unto Goshen." That Jacob should send Judah before him, to receive from Joseph the necessary orders for the reception of those entering the country, is entirely in accordance with the regulations of a well-organized kingdom, whose borders a wandering tribe is not permitted to pass unceremoniously. This account also agrees accurately with the information furnished on this point by the Egyptian monuments. That Jacob did not obtain the orders of Joseph until he was at Goshen, shows that this was the border-land. We come to the same result also from chap. xlvii. 1. "And Joseph came and told Pharaoh, and said, My father and my brethren are come out of the land of Canaan, and behold they are in the land of Goshen." It is most natural that they should remain in the border province until the matter was laid before the king. This is also confirmed by Gen. xlvi. 34: "And ye shall say, Thy servants' trade hath been about cattle, from our youth even until now; that ye may dwell in the land of Goshen; for every shepherd is an abomination unto the Egyptians;" for this passage can only be explained on the supposition that Goshen is a frontier province, which could be assigned to the Israelites, without placing them in close contact with the Egyptians, who hated their manner of life. Finally, the circumstance that the Israelites under Moses, after they had assembled at the principal town of the land, had reached in two days the confines of the Arabian desert, points to Goshen as the eastern boundary.

On the *other hand*, Goshen appears again as lying in the neighborhood of the chief city of Egypt. Thus in Gen. xlv. 10: "And thou shalt dwell in the land of Goshen, and thou shalt be near to me" (to Joseph, who dwelt in the principal city of Egypt). The Pentateuch nowhere expressly mentions which was this chief city of Egypt, just as the surname of no one of the reigning Pharaohs is mentioned by Moses, and for the same reason. Yet the necessary data for designating this city are found. It must, at any rate, have been situated in Lower Egypt, for this appears in the Pentateuch generally as the seat of the Egyptian king. But the remarkable passage, Numbers xiii. 23: "And Hebron was built seven years before Zoan of Egypt," points us directly to Zoan or Tanis, and at the same time plainly shows that the reason why the author did not mention the chief city by name can be sought in any thing rather than in his ignorance concerning it. That Zoan is here directly named by way of comparison, implies, first, that it was one of the oldest cities in Egypt. Secondly, that it held the first rank among the Egyptian cities, and stood in the most important connection with the Israelites. Hebron, the city of the patriarch, could be made more conspicuous only by a comparison with the chief city of Egypt, arrogant and proud of its antiquity; and there was no motive for such a comparison, except with a city which by its arrogance had excited the jealousy of the Israelites. The designation, Zoan of Egypt, which means more than that the city lay in Egypt, also indicates that this was the chief city. What is here only intimated is expressly affirmed in Psalm lxxviii. 12, 43, where it is said, Moses performed his wonders "in the field of Zoan." In accordance with the foregoing intimations, which bring us into the chief city, Moses is exposed on the bank of the Nile, Exodus ii. 3; and at the place where the king's daughter was accustomed to bathe, verse 5; and the mother of the child lived in the immediate vicinity, verse 8. They had fish in abundance, Num. xi. 5; they watered their land as a garden of herbs, Deut. xi. 10.

Further, the land of Goshen, on the one hand, is described as a *pasture* ground. So in the passage above referred to, Gen. xlvi.

84, and also in chap. xlvii. 4: "They said moreover unto Pharaoh, To sojourn in the land are we come; for thy servants have no pasture for their flock; for the famine is sore in the land of Canaan; now therefore we pray thee let thy servants dwell in the land of Goshen."

On the other hand, the land of Goshen appears as one of the most fruitful regions of Egypt; chap. xlvii. 6: "In the best of the land make thy father and brethren to dwell." Also in verse 11 of the same chapter: "And he gave them a possession in the land of Egypt, in the best of the land, in the land of Rameses." The Israelites employed themselves in agriculture, Deut. xi. 10; and obtained in rich abundance, Num. xi. 5, the products which Egypt, fertilized by the Nile, afforded its inhabitants.

All these circumstances harmonize, and the different points, discrepant as they may seem, find their application, when we fix upon the land of Goshen as the region east of the Tanitic arm of the Nile, as far as the Isthmus of Suez, or the border of the Arabian desert, Ex. xiii. 20. Goshen then comprised a tract of country very various in its nature. A great part of it was a barren land, suitable only for the pasturage of cattle. Yet it also had very fruitful districts, so that it combined in itself the peculiarities of Arabia and Egypt. To it belonged a part of the land on the eastern shore of the Tanitic branch of the Nile; also the whole of the Pelusiac branch, with both its banks, which, as late as the time of Alexander the Great, was navigable — through it his fleet pressed into Egypt — but is now almost entirely filled up with the sand of the desert; while the Tanitic arm, being further removed from the desert, has sustained itself better. Between two branches of the Pelusiac canal lies the island Mycephoris, which, in ancient times, was inhabited by the Calasiries, or a part of the military caste. Of this island Ritter says:—"At this present time it is a well-cultivated plain, full of great palm-groves and opulent villages." "Generally," continues the same author, "the country here is by no means barren; the water of the canal diffuses its blessings everywhere. Thus there lies upon the canal, about fifteen miles below Bustah, the little modern village Heyeh, surrounded by rich palm-groves, which is almost entirely unknown to recent geographers; but in its vicinity is a luxuriance of vegetation which makes the country appear like a European garden." So is it even now with this region, notwithstanding the great bogs and sand-heaps which have been here formed in the course of a hundred years. Even in the interior of the ancient land of Goshen there is still a large tract of land good for tillage, and fruitful. There is, for example, a valley which stretches through the whole breadth of this province from west to east, and in which, as we shall hereafter see, the ancient chief city of this province lay. This tract of land, from the ancient Babastes, on the Pelusiac arm of the Nile, even to the entrance of the Wady Tumilat, is, according to Le Père, even now under full cultivation, and is annually overflowed by the Nile. Also a great part of Wady Tumilat is susceptible of cultivation, and likewise the eastern part of the valley, which is very accurately delineated upon the chart of Lower Egypt, in the atlas of Ritter's geography, the tract from Ras el Wady to Serapeum, furnishes not merely pasture grounds, but also land suitable for cultivation.

It is certain that the Pentateuch in the intimations, evidently undesigned, which it gives of the position and nature of the land of Goshen in the most disconnected passages, is always consistent with itself; as, for example, in one whole series of passages it alludes to the fact that the Israelites dwelt upon the Nile, and in another that they dwelt in a border land in the direction of Arabia. This fact, as also the circumstance that all its allusions to the position and nature of the land are substantiated by actual geography, without the most distant reference to an imaginary land, are not explicable, if the author was dependent on uncertain reports for his information. On the contrary, the whole serves to impress us with the conviction that he, as would be the case with Moses, wrote from personal observation, with the freedom and confidence of one to whom the information communicated naturally and of its own accord, and from one who has not obtained it for a proposed object.

Hengstenberg, speaking of the genealogical table in Genesis, remarks,—

It has often been asserted that the genealogical table in Gen. x., can not be from Moses; since so extended a knowledge of nations lies far beyond the geographical horizon of the Mosaic age. This hypothesis must now be considered as exploded. The new discoveries and investigations in Egypt have shown that they maintained even from the most ancient times a vigorous commerce with other nations, and sometimes with very distant nations. The proofs are found in Creuzer, Heeren, in my contributions, and in Wilkinson. This last author, among other things, remarks, that the strongest proof for the commerce of the Egyptians with distant nations of Asia, is furnished by the materials out of which many of the articles in use, in civil and domestic use, found in the tombs of Thebes, which belong to the 18th or 19th dynasty, are made in Egypt; for example, — the vessels of wood, which are commonly made of foreign wood, and not seldom of the mahogany of India. But not merely in general do the investigations in Egyptian antiquities favor the belief that Moses was the author of the account in the tenth chapter of Genesis. On the Egyptian monuments, those especially which represent the conquests of the ancient Pharaohs over foreign nations—conquests which, certainly, were oftener achieved in imagination than in reality, as indeed the almost regular occurrence of these representations under nearly all the ancient Pharaohs shows, so that nothing can be more erroneous than the present popular way of relying upon them without inquiry, as sources of historical truth—not a few names have been found which correspond with those contained in the chapter before us. We will here speak only of those where the agreement is perfectly certain. It must be allowed that far more still could be effected if our knowlege of hieroglyphics were not so very imperfect.

Among the sons of Japheth (in verse 2), Meshech and Tiras are mentioned in close connection. Among the Asiatic nations which are represented on the monuments as engaged in war with the Egyptians, the Toersha also appear, according to Wilkinson. They are shown, indeed, among the nations who are said to have been conquered by the third Rameses. Their identity with Tiras is the less doubtful, since another nation, the Mashoash, is named along with them. These last, Wilkinson designates as "another Asiatic nation who resemble the former in their general features, and the shape of their beards." The agreement between Meshech and Tiras on the one side, and Mashoash and Toersba on the other, is the less exposed to suspicion, since Wilkinson did not think to place both in connection, as indeed in general, the present attempt at comparing the names of the people represented on the monuments with those found in Gen. x. is the first.

Among the sons of Japheth (in the same verse), Javan — the Ionians, or Greeks — is mentioned. According to Rosellini, the Uoinin (the Ionians) are found among others, in a symbolic painting, representing king Menephthah I., the 12th king of the 18th dynasty, as in the sight of Amon-re he slays one individual of each of the conquered nations. These same people were also mentioned on the monuments which belong to Thothmes V.

Among the sons of Gomer, the son of Japhet, consequently, as a Japhetic nation, Riphat is mentioned in verse 3, probably identical with the Pouônt, or Pount, who are represented on the monuments as engaged in war with the Egyptians, as early as the time of Amun-m-gori II., which the more recent chronologers place at about the year 1680 B.C.

Among the sons of Ham (in verse 5), Cush is first mentioned. The Cush, according to Wilkinson, are represented among the African people who are conquered by the monarchs of the eighteenth or nineteenth dynasty. "These" (the Cush), he remarks, "were long at war with the Egyptians; and a part of their country, which was reduced at a very remote period by the arms of the Pharaohs, was obliged to pay an annual tribute to the conquerors." According to Rosellini, the victory of King Horus over the same people, is represented on a monument at Selsilis. According to the same author, they appear in the painting already referred to, among the nations conquered by Menephthah I. Eleven separate Cushite tribes are there mentioned in agreement with verse 7, according to which Cush is not the name of a separate tribe, but of several tribes belonging to one general family.

As the second son of Ham, the second Hamitish head of a family, Mizraim is mentioned. This name was, as the dual form signifies, originally the name of the land. The division of the land into the upper and lower regions to which it refers, appears on the monuments even in the most ancient times. In proof of this, see Wilkinson and Champollion's "Letters," where an inscription is quoted, "I give thee the upper and the lower Egypt, in order that you may rule over them as king."

According to verse 13, Mizraim was the progenitor among other nations, of the Lehabim and Naphtuhim. It serves for a confirmation of the statement that the Lybians (the Lehabim) are an offshoot from the Egyptians, that they, even to the time of the Ptolemies, were considered a part of the Egyptians. Champollion affirms, that he found Niphaiat (= Naphtuchin) on the monuments as a name of Lybian nations.

The Canaanites and Amorites (called Asmaori) are represented on the Egyptian monuments with Lemanon (the people of Lebanon) and Ascalon. The land Canana is specifically named among the inscriptions upon a representation of the triumph of Menephthah I., together with the region of Nahareina or Mesopotamia, and Singara or Sincar. In reference to a representation of a campaign of Osirei, the father of Rameses the Great, Wilkinson says, "The country of Lemanon is shown by the artist to have been mountainous, inaccessible to chariots, and abounding in lofty trees, which the affrighted mountaineers are engaged in felling, in order to impede the march of the invading army. The Egyptian monarch, having taken by assault the fortified towns on the frontier, advances with the light infantry in pursuit of the fugitives, who had escaped and taken shelter in the woods, and sending a herald to offer terms on condition of their surrender; the chiefs are induced to trust to his clemency, and return to their allegiance, as are those of Canana, whose strongholds yield in like manner to the arms of the conqueror." It is readily seen from these representations, with what justice an argument against the Pentateuch has been derived from the knowledge of Canana which its author exhibits.

"The sons of Shem," it is said, in verse 22, "are Elam, and *Asshur*, and Arphaxad, and *Lud*, and Aram."

It is in the highest degree probable that Asshur appears on the monuments under the name Shari. That the Shari, who especially under the reign of Osirei and his son Rameses the Great, are represented as engaged in war with the Egyptians, are the Assyrians, is indicated not only by the name but by the similarity of dress between them and the captives of Tirhaka.

The Ludim act a conspicuous part on the Egyptian monuments. In a representation of a triumph of Menephthah I., five foreign nations are found — the Romenen, the Seios, the people Ots, from the land of Omar; the Tohen, and the Seeto. All of these, with the exception of Ots, are represented in the inscriptions as belonging to the land of Ludim. And of the whole expedition it is repeatedly said, that it was directed against the people of the land of Ludim, which is in accordance with the Book of Genesis, in which likewise Lud is not represented as a single tribe, but as an entire nation.

Since in these same inscriptions the land of Canana is also named, and the region of Nahareina and Singara, just as in Genesis Lud is closely connected with Aram, Rosellini argues that the land Ludim lay in the neighborhood of Canana and Mesopotamia, and he asserts that it must be sought in the western part of Asia.

Every reader must see the force of these scattered illustrations. These varied references prove in every case, first, that Moses must have been personally acquainted with the geography, habits, and customs of the Egyptian people of the time in which he lived. Secondly, that he has accurately described scenes and persons proved by the monuments to have been what he says they were, and therefore that he had been a resident in Egypt. Third, that therefore the charge adduced by the Bishop of Natal — that Moses probably never existed, that if he did, he was not the author of the Pentateuch, and that, whoever was the author, he states fancies for facts, and idle traditions as truth — is unfounded. The very stones cry out against the conclusions of the Bishop of Natal, and protest with a thousand tongues that Moses is right, and Dr. Colenso wrong.

How marvelous that Providence directed Champollion and Young to the Rosetta Stone, and thus disclosed the key that unlocks and the law that deciphers inscriptions three thousand years old! How marvelous that the Egyptians were led to inscribe in indelible letters on the rocks and stones the leading events and scenes of their history and social life! How marvelous that in the nineteenth century the very stones that were engraved in the days of Abraham, Isaac, and Jacob, should be laid bare in the light of day!

I am told that it is impossible to turn this Bishop out of the episcopacy which he has desecrated and perverted; and therefore it becomes the more obligatory upon every one who, like myself, has turned his attention to the claim of the Bible, as I was forced to do a good many years ago, to bring forward the irresistible evidences that the worthy Bishop is utterly mistaken; that either through ignorance, or rashness, or from some other reason I can not explain, he has made assertions which are directly untrue, and which can be proved to be untrue; and that when the comparison is fairly and impartially made, the old fact will stand out clear as the stars in the sky, God's Word, from the Pentateuch to the Apocalypse, is plain, indestructible, historic truth. Sooner may Canute repel the advancing tide; sooner may Xerxes control the Hellespont by casting a chain across its waters; sooner may Caligula command the clouds with success not to rain down upon his royal head, than priest or prelate, Bishop of Natal or Bishop of Rome, shake the solid foundations of that blessed book which, as Locke has said, and I have often repeated, has God for its author, truth without any mixture of alloy for its matter, and the present and the eternal happiness of mankind for its issue.

I look upon these illustrative facts as most important. They prove to the school of Colenso that Moses not only taught the way to heaven, as the gospels inform us, but that all he has stated in his pictures of men, in his sketches of events, in his references to Egypt, in his portraits of character, in his history of incidents, and acts, and revolutions, is historically true; that all his writings are, from beginning to end, what our reformers, and our confessors, and articles declare — canonical Scriptures, preaching Christ, and teaching the way to the Father.

CHAPTER XI.

FURTHER MONUMENTAL WITNESSES TO MOSES.

It has been asserted in the highest quarters, and not by a solitary individual, but by many who belong to the same school, that Moses is not a reliable annalist of facts; that what he states as historic events never occurred; that the Pentateuch is to a great extent a composite of fables, traditions, romances, fancies; that there is no reason to believe that Moses was inspired to write what is not true; and that he is not to be accepted as a credible and authentic historian. We have already seen that Moses preaches Christ, and must have been inspired to sketch a photograph of one that came into the world 1,500 years afterwards. We have seen that the Saviour gives His attestation to Moses. We have also gathered from the Egyptian monuments some proofs of the authenticity of the Pentateuch.

We will now present a few additional illustrative facts in the same direction. Suppose Moses is silent, the stones of the monuments, the sarcophagi of the Pharaohs, the last resting-places of a thousand mummies, signet rings from the beds of rivers, seals from the ruins of ancient Babylon and buried Nineveh, all come up and silently exhibit, substantially, allusions to those very events which the Bishop of Natal says are not true. So that if he will not hear Moses, he may perhaps be persuaded when dead kings rise from their graves and attest what Moses said; he may also hear, though none are so deaf as those that won't hear, the very stones crying out that Moses is right, and the Bishop utterly and disastrously wrong.

We find the whole valley of Sinai, in the Sinaitic Peninsula, covered with stones on which are what seem to be remarkable inscriptions of events and scenes that have passed away. A Bishop of the Church of Ireland offered £500 to any one that would decipher them. Several experiments have been made, some with more success than others. It is at least singular that the very scene where God Almighty wrote with His finger on the hard granite the Ten Commandments of the Law, should also be the scene of rocks covered with inscriptions in symbolic characters, and in many cases in a language we have not been able to penetrate. In the account of the Law it is stated in Exodus xxxi. 18; "And God gave unto Moses, when he had made an end of communing with him upon Mount Sinai, two tables of testimony, tables of stone, written with the finger of God." We also read that Moses, when he came down from the mount, and heard the shouts of the people, let the slabs fall; the weight, one would suppose, can not have been very great; and they were broken to pieces. I stated, in a previous lecture, that it is just possible that the ark may be found still remaining in the clefts of Ararat, having settled in the hollow between the two mountain peaks, when there was no snow; for if any, it had been swept away by the Flood; and then the snow, and the ice, and the avalanche having accumulated above it thousands of feet in depth, never yet penetrated by man;—it is just possible, that in such intensely low temperature decay may be completely arrested. But what a startling discovery, if the Bishop of Natal were yet to live to hear that the remains of the ark have been discovered on Ararat! Its voice would surely penetrate the most impenetrable ear, and he would renounce and repent of his rash assertion that the Flood is a myth, and the ark a delusion and a dream. In the same manner, it is perfectly possible—I do not say there is much chance of the discovery—that the very stones—the broken stones on which the finger of the Almighty engraved in imperishable sculpture the living and the lasting laws of morality, of righteousness, may yet be found. Mount Sinai gives no evidence whatever of having been the scene, the recent scene, of volcanic eruption; it is composed of granite, as stated by travelers, of the most beautiful and valuable description; and granite stones have been successively taken from it; and on those stones there are inscriptions, copies of which I have seen, partly in Arabic letters, partly in broken Samaritan Hebrew, and partly in unknown characters; and though £500 have been offered for deciphering them, no one seems to have yet earned the reward. One of them, however, has been deciphered by the Rev. C. Forster, a clergyman of the Church of England, who copied several inscriptions found upon the rocks — some not on the granite, but on the red sandstone, on the route from Suez to Sinai; and one of them contains the first line of the blessing that Aaron was commanded to pronounce upon the children of Israel. It is translated literally from the Arabic, "The everlasting Jehovah bless thee." Now, a Mahometan can not have sculptured it, for it is older than the era of Mahomet. It is not probable that a Christian did so. It may be a fragment of a rock on which the Aaronitic blessing was engraved, the most familiar benediction in all the usage of the ancient religious ritual of Israel: "The Lord bless thee and keep thee; the Lord make his face to shine upon thee and be gracious unto thee; the Lord lift up the light of his countenance upon thee, and give thee peace."

But I turn to some stones at present of far more pertinent and relative significance. We read, for instance, in 2 Kings xvii. 5, "Then the king of Assyria came up throughout all the land, and went up to Samaria, and besieged it three years. In the ninth year of Hoshea the king of Assyria took Samaria, and carried Israel away into Assyria, and placed them in Halah and in Habor by the river of Gozan, and in the cities of the Medes." Here is the record, given by inspiration, of the beginning of the captivity of the ten tribes —a record which is not admitted to be historical by the Bishop to whom I have referred, but supposed to be apocryphal. If the Bishop disbelieves Moses, let him hear the rocks. We find this captivity of the ten tribes confirmed by discoveries of inscriptions that have been sculptured on the rock. I have seen an engraving descriptive of the occurrence of this very captivity of the ten tribes, in a gang of captives tied by a rope round the neck of each, moving in line, one behind the other. The king of Assyria stands receiving them; his right foot is trampling upon the breast of one poor captive, who throws up his hands in agony. Other seven or eight follow in succession, tied one to the other by a continuous rope; their countenances unmistakably Jewish, for the Jewish type is visible upon every feature. It is a singular fact, that all the monumental inscriptions of Egypt are real pictures, exact and true miniatures, of acts of persons that actually lived. And the last of the captives in the gang, if I may use the phrase, has a miter on his head, indicating that he belonged to the house of Levi, and was a Jewish priest. Sir Robert Ker Porter concludes from this, that the sculpture undoubtedly refers to the conquest of Israel and the captivity of the ten tribes by Shalmaneser, king of Assyria and of the Medes. Suppose that the Bishop should deny that the book of Kings contains history, let him read the monuments, let him hear the stones crying out in eloquent protest, God's Word is truth.

I notice another incident illustrative of the same. A signet has been found in the ruins of ancient Babylon, amidst the brick and *débris* of the ancient tower of Babel, representing (I have seen the engraving of it) a victorious charioteer standing in his chariot. Before him is a lion, wounded by two or three arrows that have been shot into his head and heart,—that lion meant to represent the lion of the tribe of Judah. And behind the lion is a palm-tree, conveying unmistakably the impression that it refers to Judea, the palm-tree being its characteristic national symbol. Here, then, you have another indirect evidence of the same fact, of which I have given already one proof. And Sir Robert Ker Porter, who records this, says that "even to this day the banks of the Euphrates are hoary with reeds, and the gray osier willow yet abounds upon its banks, on some of which the captives of Israel hung their harps when they remembered Zion."

Let me mention another confirmatory incident. We read in 2 Chronicles xii. 9, "So Shishak, king of Egypt, came up against Jerusalem, and took away the treasures of the house of the Lord, and the treasures of the king's house;" and this occurred in the reign of Rehoboam, the son of Solomon, who became tributary to Shishak. It is stated in the book of Chronicles that Rehoboam was taken captive, that the treasures of the house of the Lord were also taken, and that Jerusalem was taken by Shishak, the king of Egypt. Is this an historical fact, or is it not? Suppose that you ignore the statement of the inspired writer, let us ask if there is any collateral or illustrative proof in the discoveries of the monuments. In a sculpture at Karnak is discovered Shishak dragging the chiefs of thirty nations. His name, inscribed in hieroglyphic characters, is Shishak; and among the captives, one engraving I have seen represents Rehoboam; and under the figure of Rehoboam, one of the captives, with a Jewish face so marked as to be ultra-Jewish, is written in hieroglyphics, *Yehuda Melek*, "The King of Judea." Now, recollect this was inscribed nearly 3,000 years ago. And what is the amount of it? Why, just this, that the very incident recorded in 2 Chronicles was recorded by an independent historian, who could have no interest in recording it, except simply to celebrate the actual triumphs and the conquests of a victorious king of Egypt; certainly not with the idea of meeting the difficulties of the Bishop of Natal, and proving that what he says is a myth is—what it does prove to be—literal and actual fact.

Mr. Murray, who has written upon this subject, says —(I do not give you the facts in any historical succession; they are so interesting and so important that each by itself is an independent witness to the historic claims of Moses and the Old Testament Scripture)— "An ancient Egyptian coin is in my possession on which are seven ears of corn, and the reaper cutting it down." Another coin also he has obtained, on which are seven ears of corn all bound together, the idea conveyed being a plentiful harvest. Now, connect that with the seven years of famine and the seven years of abundance, under Joseph in Egypt, and you have, if not a conclusive, at least a highly probable reference to the famine and the plenty; at all events to the usages of speaking in the land of Egypt.

Another interesting fact is that stated by Belzoni. I have seen the engraving he describes. He found in the tomb of one of the ancient Egyptian kings the engraving of an ark of bulrushes floating up the Nile, and in the ark an infant with a hawk's head,—the Egyptian way of representing the highest wisdom; and therefore the idea taught by the bulrush ark floating on the Nile, with an infant in it, seated, with a hawk head instead of a human head, is simply this, that some child of marvelous wisdom had been preserved in an ark of bulrushes, floating on the Nile. Turn to the Book of Exodus, and what the Bishop calls a myth we find recorded upon the monumental stones of Egypt; by people that never believed in the Bible, nor cared any thing about its claims; but whose independent testimony at the present time is of incalculable value.

Let me pass on a little later to some other interesting illustrations. We are Protestants, and we ought to be able to give a reason for the faith that is in us; and the reason is so overwhelming, and the force of proof so triumphant, that I can not do better than rivet in your memory these most important and suggestive facts. Sir Robert Ker Porter, to whom I have alluded, and Mr. Kettle, have collected illustrative inscriptions, of events and circumstances in the history of Daniel. Now, the Book of Daniel is one of the books that the rationalists have waged exterminating war against. The fact is, these people do not like prophecy at all, and they especially dislike doing what I have always tried to do, and what, by God's grace, I mean to do—taking every word of prophecy as God's inspired record, and holding it just as God has given it, as the word of truth. But they say it is all myth, and romance ; and they prefer to dilute it and explain it away, till at last it is evaporated into myths and metaphors the most extravagant and airy. Sir Robert Ker Porter says, "There is a block of gray granite which has been discovered in the western palace of Babylon, which probably crowned one of the gates of the palace of the king of Babylon. On this block of gray granite is a huge lion, standing over the prostrate figure of a man, who is crushed by it." There is no record ; there is simply the picture. Also, the same authority says, "They fished up from the bed of the river Euphrates, on which Babylon stood, various silver coins. On the reverse of the coins are castellated buildings, each of them over dens of lions ;" certainly so far illustrative and allusive. "On the obverse of one of the coins is a man in mortal conflict with a lion." On the obverse of another coin is the figure of a man, his features those of a Jew. He is standing with a foot upon each of two sphinxes that look up; while two lions stand erect, one on the right and the other on the left; he takes the paw of one with his right hand, and the paw of the other with his left hand, and seems to be in perfect safety, or to be the sovereign ruler of the wild and ferocious beasts. I do not say there is any inscription; but read the story of Daniel, and the mode of punishment by lions in his day; read his personal immunity in the lion's den, and you can not fail to infer if this be not an actual picture of Daniel laying his hands upon the fierce brutes, and the animals touched by One higher than he, feeling friendship, and resting in peace; and if not the very representative thing itself, illustrative at least of some fact very much like it, and analogous to it. There is another stone, very remarkable, a relic of Susa—and you recollect Daniel was governor of Susa as well as governor of Babylon. Sir Robert Ker Porter thus describes it: "It does not exceed ten inches in width and depth, and measures twenty inches in length. It is hollow within, as if to receive some deposit. Three of its sides are cut in bas relief; two of them have similar representations of a man apparently naked except a sash round his waist, and a sort of cap upon his head. His hands are bound behind him. The corner of the stone forms the neck of the figure. Two lions, in sitting postures, appear on each side at the top, having each a paw upon his head." Read the account of Daniel, bound, and cast into the lions' den; and you have upon the stone an illustration of the very fact recorded in the Book of Daniel, and the strongest possible presumption, therefore, that Daniel records what is historic and literal truth.

I pass on to another incident, illustrative of another event in the history of Daniel; and after that, I will revert to the Pentateuch. There was found, it appears in the ruins of Babylon, a coin which is in the possession of a gentleman of the name of Burgoyne. On this coin are engraven three figures of men in a burning furnace. Outside the furnace is a hideous and gigantic idol; and round the idol are two or three people worshiping and giving homage to it. Read the story of the three Hebrew youths, the furnace and the idol on Dura; and recollect, these coins, fished from the bed of the Euphrates, are not one of them less than, probably, 2,500 years old, and must be descriptive of contemporaneous or memorable historic facts. So that not only the stones on the wall, the rocks in the desert, but the very river throws up its buried treasures, and it is my privilege to bring forward the facts, to demonstrate to you how absurdly, how rashly, how unphilosophically—to take the faintest estimate of his conduct—the unhappy Bishop has spoken who states that these events recorded in Scripture are not facts, but myths, and fancies, and delusions.

The Rev. Mr. Saville, from whom I have often quoted, states the following incident. The book from which he draws his extracts is Lepsius, who was employed and paid all his expenses by the Prussian Government, to take drawings of what he found upon the Egyptian monuments; and he has done it in the most perfect way. The book is in the British Museum, where you can easily see it. I am no German scholar, otherwise I would have copied the extracts from it for myself; but those who speak German will be able no doubt to enjoy very much the reading of the work. The Rev. Mr. Saville, who copies from it, says, "Between the reigns of Chebron, Amenophis I., and his successor Tuthmosis the First, there was a regency in Egypt, when Amessis, or Sesamen, as it reads in the hieroglyphics, the daughter of Amosis, governed either in her own right, or in behalf of a younger relation." On an obelisk of granite erected by her at Thebes, which is one of the most splendid monuments of that country, she bears, among other titles, such as "royal wife," "royal sister," the significant one, "Pharaoh's daughter;" the only occurrence of such a name given to any female among the hieroglyphics and on the monuments. We find that this very same regency was cotemporaneous with the era and birth of Moses. This seems, therefore, to show that this lady, not having children of her own, adopted Moses after she had preserved him from the effect of Pharaoh's cruel edict; and that, in consequence of the subsequent refusal of Moses to mount the throne of Egypt—choosing affliction with the people of God rather than the pleasures of sin for a season; preferring the reproach of Israel to the riches of Egypt—the throne passed to Tuthmosis the First, who appears upon the monuments as the son of Amosis, but was probably only a near kinsman. I do not say that the demonstration is perfect; but here is the remarkable coïncidence that, at the birth of Moses, a woman inter-reigned; that woman is described on the monuments as "Pharaoh's daughter"—the very phrase that the apostle Paul and Moses apply to her. We find that she, after her interregnum, was succeeded by a distant kinsman; that she had no children; that she adopted Moses, whom she meant to be a Pharaoh, and king of Egypt, who, however, preferred the reproach of Christ to the riches of Egypt; a choice that he never repented of on earth, and repents not of now in heaven. Is it not highly probable that this is the very Pharaoh's daughter that clasped the babe in her bosom, nourished him, taught him the wisdom of Egypt, would have made him king; though he, inspired by a heavenly influence, and actuated by a sublimer motive, preferred the desert with allegiance to his God, to the splendid palatial glory of Pharaoh with denial of that Jesus in whom he believed?

Let me notice another incident, also very striking. It is this. Dr. Hincks has discovered, and not very long ago, on the Nimroud obelisk, the following name, "Jehu, the son of Omri." The very inscription on the rocks is the repetition of the name in

Scripture; and it proves this, at least, that Israel and Assyria must have had some connection, seeing that an Israelitish name is engraved upon an Assyrian rock, and so far justifying the record of the captivity of the ten tribes.

What is said in Scripture of Hezekiah being vanquished by Sennacherib, has been found by Layard, the present member for the borough of Southwark, on the rock. It has been subsequently translated by Sir Henry Rawlinson. It is an inscription of the annals of his reign on the palace of Luxor. The Scripture incident recorded in it, is found in 2 Kings xviii. 13, and I wish particularly to notice the Scripture words, in order that you may see how perfectly parallel is the hieroglyphic record. "Now, in the fourteenth year of king Hezekiah did Sennacherib, king of Assyria, come up against all the fenced cities of Judah, and took them. And Hezekiah, king of Judah, sent to the king of Assyria, to Lachish, saying, I have offended; return from me: that which thou puttest on me will I bear;" that is, the tribute thou exactest I will pay. "And the king of Assyria appointed unto Hezekiah king of Judah, three hundred talents of silver, and thirty talents of gold;" that is, he levied this amount from him after he had submitted to his supremacy. "And Hezekiah gave him all the silver that was found in the house of the Lord, and in the treasures of the king's house. At that time did Hezekiah cut off the gold from the doors of the temple of the Lord, and from the pillars which Hezekiah, king of Judah, had overlaid, and gave it to the king of Assyria."

When Hezekiah submitted to the king of Assyria, and consented to give whatever tribute the king of Assyria would exact from him, he gave him, first, three hundred talents of silver, and thirty talents of gold; but we read, also, that he gave him, in addition to this, "all the silver that was found in the house of the Lord." He gave first, thirty talents of gold—that is specified; but in addition to the three hundred talents of silver, he gave him an immense quantity of silver found in the house of the Lord.

Let us now read the following record inscribed upon one of the monuments. The Ninevite inscription has been strictly and exactly deciphered by Sir Henry Rawlinson; and here it is, not, mark you, written by a Christian, nor by a Jew; but written by a heathen upward of 2,500 years ago, and therefore of unquestionable authenticity, and of great value. Here is the hieroglyphic inscription. "Because Hezekiah, king of Judah, did not submit to my yoke, forty of his strong fenced cities, and innumerable smaller towns which depended upon them, I took and plundered; but I left to Hezekiah, Jerusalem, his capital city, and some of the smaller towns around it. Because Hezekiah still refused to pay me homage I attacked him, and carried off the whole population which dwelt around Jerusalem, with thirty talents of gold, and eight hundred talents of silver — the accumulated wealth of the nobles of Hezekiah's court; and of their daughters and of the officers of his palace, men-slaves and women-slaves, I carried to Nineveh; and I accounted in the spoil my tribute which he refused to pay me."

Now, just notice the striking coïncidence. First of all, the historic facts as engraved on the monuments, are almost the translation into other words of the Scripture record in the Second Book of Kings. But you notice, in the Second Book of Kings, it reads — "thirty talents of gold and three hundred talents of silver," while it is also stated, that other silver was added. And, accordingly, we find the king, Sennacherib, giving the account of the sum total of the whole to be eight hundred talents of silver; that is, the three hundred talents paid, and the additional silver which Hezekiah says he paid him from the house of the Lord; an undesigned coïncidence that most clearly proves the authenticity of the fact, and shows again the very stones crying out from Babylon, from Nineveh, from Egypt — Moses is right, and his writing historical.

There is every reason to believe that the Birs Nimroud, the remains of which you may see engraved in any ordinary book of Scripture antiquity, was the temple of Belus, and the tower of ancient Babel.

Mr. Buckingham describes it as "a pyramid of

eight separate stages, rising and retreating within each other."

Herodotus, the ancient Greek historian, whose veracity is generally admitted, states, that the temple of Belus was the tower of Babel.

Mr. Rich, alluding to its ruins, says, "As seen at present, it is cloven by a deep furrow; the other parts, to the summit of the pyramid, are occupied by immense fragments of brickwork, tumbled together, and converted into solid vitrified masses; as if it had undergone the action of the fiercest fire, or as if it had been blown up by gunpowder."

Sir Robert Ker Porter says, "In this pyramid, we see the very tower of Babel, the stupendous monument executed by Nimroud upon the plains of Shinar."

Now, you will remember, when men began to build that tower, about the identity of which I have no doubt, they were of one language, and they meant it to be a monument of impious unbelief. God had said, As long as you see that beautiful bow span the blue firmament, or spread itself upon the black thunder-cloud, so long there shall not be another flood.

Here I state what will be set down by some of the newspapers as perfect fanaticism; but, if it be fanaticism, it is my faith. I am just as certain that another flood will not overwhelm the earth as I am certain of the existence of God Almighty himself. And the ground of my belief is, that God said, I will put my bow in the clouds, and as long as you see that bow so long be assured there will not be another universal flood. Now, if that be fanaticism in the estimate of some, it is sober scriptural faith in the judgment of God. The natives of the plain of Shinar disbelieved the pledge in the bow: they repudiated the sacramental sign; they thought they would lay down a means of safety far better than God's Word; they built this gigantic tower; so that they said, if the water should rise as high as Ararat, 17,000 feet, we will build a tower higher than Ararat, so that the water shall never be able to reach us. It was mere physical force and skill pitted against the Word of God. God was so grieved at this want of confidence in His Word, and this attempt to supersede it, that it is said He looked down; and their speech was cloven, and broken into dialects. And the word "looking down" often means in Scripture, nay, generally means in Scripture, visiting with judgments; and the probability is that the lightnings of heaven tore the fabric into fragments, and that the vitrified brick and the rent ruins are the standing traces of the righteous judgments of God. Of this there is evidence, apart altogether from Scripture. To this historic fact Dr. Wiseman refers. It is a strange thing to be constrained to quote a Roman Catholic Bishop against a Protestant Bishop; but in this instance the Roman Catholic Bishop is the better of the two. Dr. Wiseman states that all ethnologists have come to this conclusion, that all languages indicate a common source; but also indicate in their historical transmission a fracture or dislocation. These are the philosophical words in which he conveys what is the judgment of ethnologists. And the most recent writer upon languages, Max Muller, a professor in the University of Oxford, says, at the conclusion of his most interesting and able work, "The science of language thus leads us up to that highest summit from which we see into the very dawn of man's life on earth, and when and where those words which we have heard so often from the days of our childhood, 'And the whole earth was of one language and one speech,' assume a meaning more natural, more intelligible, and more convincing than we ever marked before." The highest science supplies the strongest evidence of the truth of the Word of God. A very able writer, speaking upon this subject, says, referring to these opponents of the Bible, "Had Voltaire been now alive he would not have ventured to put the sneering question, how and out of what materials the Hebrew lawgiver could write the Pentateuch;" a question, by the by, that the Bishop of Natal borrows from him; "for," says this writer, "it is proved that the papyrus was in common use for writing in his day; nor would he have tauntingly asked how, after an interval of a thousand years, Hilkiah could find in the temple of Jerusalem the autograph of the law; for writings and contracts on papyrus as old as the days of Pharaoh still exist, and are still legible. Nor would he have insinuated against Ezra the charge of having forged the Sacred Books." Voltaire is not half so bad as the Bishop of Natal in this respect; because the Bishop of Natal says, it was Samuel that wrote the Pentateuch, and that he collected a lot of floating traditions and fables, and pieced them together. Voltaire did not go so far as that. We know that Ezra did collect and arrange the Sacred Books, and probably added here and there, what we can detect, the modern name of an ancient city. Ezra, however, was an inspired man. Voltaire admitted that Ezra did so; but he says that Ezra forged the books, which is a very different thing. "Nor would he have insinuated against Ezra the charge of having forged the Sacred Books which he collected; for the written and monumental history of Egypt so coïncides with these books in dates and facts as to show that they were not the work of imposture." And Benjamin Constant, an eminent French writer, well says: "He who would be gay with Voltaire, at the expense of Ezekiel and Genesis, must unite two things, which will make his gayety sufficiently melancholy; ignorance the most profound, and frivolity the most deplorable."

And let me give, in drawing these remarks to a close, a most impressive extract from a sermon preached by one, with whose ecclesiastical sentiments in many respects I do not agree — for High Churchism, I think, has just its reäction in Rationalism — I mean the present eloquent Bishop of Oxford. He says, in one of his sermons, most eloquently and impressively, "I can tell you of an overshadowing grave which closed in on such a struggle and such an end"—the doubter's end he is speaking of—"as that at which I have glanced. In it was laid a form that had hardly reached the fullness of earliest manhood. That young man had gone, young, ardent, and simply faithful, into the tutelage of one, himself I doubt not, a sincere believer, but who sought to reconcile the teachings of the Protestant Church, in which he ministered, with the dreams of Rationalism. His favorite pupil learnt his lore, and it sufficed for his needs while health beat high in his youthful veins. But on him sickness and decay closed early in; and as the glow of health failed, the intellectual lights for which he had exchanged the simplicity of faith began to pale; whilst the viper brood of doubts which almost unawares he had let slip into his soul, crept forth from their hiding-places, and raised against him fearfully their envenomed heads. They were too strong for him; the teacher who had suggested the doubts could not remove them, and in darkness and despair his victim died before his eyes—the doubter."

Meanwhile, let us rejoice that the stone calls out from the walls, "Thy word, O God, is truth." The dead mummy wakes from its long and its heavy sleep; rises from its wooden coffin; holds the imperishable papyrus in its hand, and on that hand the eye of the nineteenth century reads, "Moses and the prophets spake truth." The sarcophagi of the ancient Egyptian kings are penetrated; the lamp of the everlasting gospel lets its light shine upon them, and we discover the solemn and sublime shadows of Moses, Abraham, Isaac, and Jacob. Shadows visible in the nineteenth century projected from the originals who lived 3,000 years before. Coins dug from the depths of the Euphrates say, "God's word is truth." Thirty centuries emerge from the shadows of the past, each century with its testimony in its hand, and that testimony is that the words of Moses are words of history and of fact. The Pharaohs in their pyramidal chambers seem to hear the sound or to feel the breath of the resurrection trumpet, and they, too, are now coming forth at the bidding of God, and each Pharaoh — most unexpected use — the very Pharaoh that persecuted Israel, and would not let Israel go; the very Pharaoh that lost his first-born amidst the judgments upon Egypt when the Exodus took place; all step forth from their cold, damp, pyramidal chambers, and each holds his testimony in his hand, and each declares, what we feel, and in our hearts we cherish, how transient is all that man thinks great; how lasting, how real, how true, is the shortest word that God has inspired in the Sacred Volume.

www.ingramcontent.com/pod-product-compliance
Lightning Source LLC
LaVergne TN
LVHW010235110826
845151LV00004B/1297

* 9 7 8 1 4 2 5 5 2 4 9 3 7 *